STRIKE
BACK

STRIKE
BACK

REDISCOVERING MILITANT TACTICS TO FIGHT THE ATTACKS ON PUBLIC EMPLOYEE UNIONS

JOE BURNS

PUBLISHING

NEW YORK, NY

Please direct inquiries to:
Ig Publishing, Inc
PO Box 2547
New York, NY 10163
www.igpub.com

ISBN 978-1-6324608-9-9

For Warren J. Burns

CONTENTS

FOREWORD

In early 2018, the United States was hit by a strike wave for the first time in decades. Hundreds of thousands of educators in red states across the country walked off their jobs to demand better school funding and better pay. In the process, these strikers not only won historic gains for themselves and their students, but they've given hope to, and pointed the way forward for, the labor movement as a whole.

This historic upsurge constitutes a direct challenge to the longstanding reliance of union officials across the country on "partnering" with management and lobbying mainstream Democrats. It also cuts against the prevailing advice of most labor scholars, among whom surprisingly few have pointed to reviving the strike as key to organized labor's revival.

In contrast, Joe Burns' 2014 book, *Strike Back: Using the Militant Tactics of Labor's Past to Reignite Public Sector Unionism Today*, has been entirely vindicated by the red state revolt. Indeed, recent events have remarkably confirmed his political analysis and his strategic prescriptions. In this preface, I sketch out how the recent strike wave has confirmed four of Burns' main arguments: the centrality of the strike; the need to break labor law; the importance of community support; and the urgency of defeating the right-wing's privatization offensive.

Reviving the Strike

When it comes to political strategy, there's no need to reinvent the wheel. The core contention of *Strike Back* is that the largely overlooked public sector worker upsurge of the 1960s and 1970s shows what it will take to reverse the fortunes of working people and unions today. Above all, this means reviving the strike.

West Virginia, Arizona, and the subsequent teacher revolts of 2018 have once again confirmed that strikes are workers' most powerful weapon. By shutting down production—whether in the private or public sector—working people have immense structural power to force employers to meet their demands. As Arizona teacher leader Dylan Wegela put it:

> A strike was the only way forward, because nothing else had worked. Electing Democrats didn't work—all across the country they've also cut school funds. But strikes work. My argument was basically: "We can win. We're the gears of the machine, if we stop showing up, everything shuts down."

Formerly an accepted commonplace, this idea was dropped decades ago by organized labor and marginalized on the Left. For both movements, the consequences of turning away from on-the-job militancy have been dire. Labor-management "cooperation" has led to concession after concession by unions across the country. The much-heralded organizing model associated with SEIU and the "New Voice" leadership that swept the AFL-CIO in the 1990s has not significantly increased union density. Nor has the prevailing form of social justice unionism reversed organized labor's decline. Even progressive unions today often remain more focused on electing and lobbying Democrats than in building workplace fightbacks.

But the teacher upsurge of 2018 shows that strikes get the goods. Though not all of their demands were met, striking educators in West Virginia, Oklahoma, and Arizona won more in the span of two months than was accomplished over the past two decades. That they wrested these concessions from intransigent Republican administrations—who for years prior stubbornly insisted that there was no money available to meet the teachers' demands—made their achievements all the more significant. Mass strikes have a remarkable knack for helping employers cough up concessions.

In West Virginia, the push for a work stoppage forced the state to withdraw its controversial rate hikes to the PEIA state health insurance plan. Then, after almost two weeks of shuttered schools, West Virginia's legislature caved to the strikers and granted a five percent raise to all public employees—not only teachers. When I spoke with rank-and-file organizer Jay O'Neal in Charleston a few hours after victory was announced, he stressed that this was the climax of an even longer string of wins:

> I'm excited, I'm thrilled, I feel like my life won't ever be the same again. It sounds like hyperbole, but it's not. And what a lot of people have already forgotten is how much we have already won. The government was forced to drop the Go365 program and to keep the PEIA insurance premiums and deductibles at their current level. Also, because of the strike, we were able to ensure that a lot of

bad education bills weren't able to get passed. The charter school bill didn't go anywhere, and additional anti-union bills like "payroll protection" all were dropped.

The gains won in Oklahoma and Arizona were also impressive. In the Sooner State, teachers won a $6,000 average pay raise by forcing the government to pass its first tax hike since 1990. In Arizona, through two months of mobilizing and six school days of striking, the Red for Ed movement put sufficient pressure on the legislature to stop new proposed tax cuts, keep an anti-voucher referendum on the 2018 ballot, and win hundreds of millions of dollars in additional school funding. Teachers, moreover, obliged the state to grant them roughly a 19 percent pay increase.

It cannot be overstressed that the achievements of the red state walkouts were not limited to the formal policy arena. Even more important than gains in pay and funding were the advances made in terms of revitalizing the trade unions and rebuilding a militant workers' movement. In particular, West Virginia and Arizona's strikes reflected, and spurred, a dramatic increase in working-class consciousness, organization, and determination to fight, setting the stage for the conquest of further victories in the months and years ahead. To quote Arizona teacher activist Rebecca Garelli:

The movement and the walkout really increased people's political awareness and our level of grassroots organization. Fifty percent of the win here has been that we now have a strong, organized mass movement. And we're not going away. People now have the courage to fight.

Arizona and West Virginia's unprecedented uptick in union dues-payers provides a quantifiable metric for the depth of this revitalization. In a marked reversal of fortunes for West Virginian organized labor, over 2,500 school employees have joined the education unions since January 2018. Arizona—in which the union represented only 25 percent of school employees in early 2018—has experienced an even deeper sea change, with over 2,750 new members joining the Arizona Education Association (AEA). On a Facebook thread concerning the lessons of the strike, a teacher explained:

> I realized how much power a group of united individuals can have when they all stand up and fight for the common good. The word "union" does not scare me anymore. I joined AEA and plan on continuing to fight for what is right for educators and students. I feel the most empowered I have ever felt as an educator and now do believe that change is possible.

Breaking the Law

As noted above, labor leaders and sympathetic scholars have put forward a wide array of proposals for reversing the fortunes of the labor movement. Most have sought either to accept, and work around, the draconian legal restrictions for organized labor in the United States, or to reform these away through legislative efforts. In contrast, Joe Burns forcefully argues that "it is not conceivable that the labor movement will be revived in any meaningful way without workers violating labor law, as their counterparts half a century ago did."[1]

Public sector strikes remain illegal in the vast majority of states in this country. Given the obvious risks of illegal workplace action, the top union officialdom in the US has been unsurprisingly hesitant to either advocate or test the strategic option of illegal workplace action. But the strikes in West Virginia and Arizona demonstrated that, for labor to win, it's both necessary and possible to break illegitimate labor laws.

Breaking the law wasn't a decision educators made lightly. Indeed, most teachers were initially highly skeptical about the potential for an illegal work stoppage. Understandably, many were concerned about losing their jobs or facing other disciplinary penalties. Music teacher Noah Karvelis recalls the situation in Arizona: "When we first started organizing, people on the Facebook group were really scared about even talking about the potential for a strike since it wasn't legal." The same was true in West Virginia, despite the state's stronger traditions of labor militancy and the precedent of an illegal teachers' strike in 1990. Lisa Collins, a teacher and union leader from Wyoming County, posted the following to the state workers' Facebook group in January: "Teachers back then [in 1990] were fearless. We don't have that today. What has happened to people?"

It took the concerted efforts of radical rank-and-file organizers to begin turning the tide. In West Virginia, the first mention of what some teachers referred to as the "s word" came on October 6, 2017 when Jay O'Neal posted news about the push towards a strike in Fresno, California. "We are settling for FAR TOO LITTLE here," O'Neal's post to the Facebook group concluded. A skeptical educator replied that "WV teachers aren't allowed to strike," to which O'Neal responded, "true, but they did anyway in 1990 and it made a big difference." Over the coming months, this basic debate was repeated thousands of times in a myriad of iterations online and offline. Eventually, the rank-and-file in both states successfully pressured their unions to get on board with the call for a strike.

High-ranking state officials and politicians responded to educators' strike authorization votes with threats of sanctions against any employee walkouts. West Virginia Attorney General Patrick Morrissey announced the following on the eve of West Virginia's action:

[A] work stoppage of any length on any ground is illegal. Let us make no mistake, the impending work stoppage is unlawful. State law and court rulings give specific parties avenues to remedy such illegal conduct, including the option to seek an injunction to end an unlawful strike.[2]

Hoping to prevent a walkout, Arizona's State Superintendent of Schools Diane Douglas similarly hit the media trail in the days leading up to the strike to threaten educators with the loss of their teaching certificate if they struck: "A walkout is a nice term for it. It is a strike, plain and simple. And in Arizona, it is not legal for teachers to strike."[3]

Ultimately, however, the state was unable to make good on its threats. The sheer number of employees on strike made the prospect of firing all strikers unfeasible. Other forms of sanctions were avoided above all for political reasons. Repression risked emboldening, rather than intimidating, the strikers and their supporters. It also risked further alienating politicians from the public.

State officials were refreshingly upfront about the political reasons underlying their reluctance to resort to legal sanctions in

2018. When asked in a post-strike press conference why he had not tried to impose an injunction, West Virginia State Superintendent Steve Paine's reply was to the point. It only would have "added gas to the fire," he acknowledged.[4] For her part, West Virginia rank-and-file leader Emily Comer summed up the lesson of the strike wave as follows: "It doesn't matter if an action is illegal if you have enough people doing it."

Community Support

Throughout *Strike Back*, Burns underscores that the nature of a public sector strike requires that employees and their organizations win over the public to their cause. What teachers lack in the ability to cut off profits, they can often make up for through their influence among broad layers of the working class. West Virginia's AFT union president Christine Campbell put it well:

> The thing that makes the public sector different is the relationships we develop. Educators are embedded in our communities; people trust us to educate their kids. So when parents see the teachers of their children struggling to make ends meet, working at a second job on the weekend, this is a much more direct relationship with the community than in the private sector.

Public education's location at the heart of social reproduction means that these work stoppages involved far more people than the roughly 130,000 teachers and support staff that struck in Arizona, Oklahoma, and West Virginia. The total number of students that missed class was well over 1.5 million; the number of affected family members roughly twice that. Even if we don't include the one-day walkouts in Kentucky, Colorado, and North Carolina, it's clear that the red state rebellions involved millions of individuals. Stakes in a system-wide school strike are high.

Aiming to win over parents and the broader public, each of the contending sides naturally sought to blame each other for the conflict. For example, a typical conservative op-ed published a few days before Arizona's strike called the impending action a "war against parents":

> As of Thursday, the fight will no longer be teachers vs. politicians; the fight will be teachers vs. parents. ... Some parents are begging friends and family to watch their kids. Others are getting prices for daycare and worrying if they'll be able to afford it on their stretched budgets.[5]

For most unions, building unity with the community has meant working with liberal NGOs to promote electoral campaigns or, at best, to organize demonstrations in support of progressive demands. Much of this work is laudatory. But as Burns has pointed out, labor's current social justice unionism approach suffers from two critical flaws. First, it has gone hand-in-hand with an abandonment of the strike weapon. Second, it has depended on alliances from on high with relatively weak nonprofits and community leaders, instead of relying on rank-and-file workers to organize and mobilize the broader working-class communities of which they are an integral part.

A different model of social justice unionism exists—one capable of generating the power required to win. The red state revolt showed what this alternative looks like in practice by leaning on the leverage of workplace militancy, raising demands on behalf of the whole working class, and tapping into strikers' deep social networks.

To win parent and student support, teachers in West Virginia began grassroots organizing months before they voted to go on strike. They took every opportunity to discuss with parents, explaining that educator working conditions were students' learning conditions. They waved signs, pass out informational fliers, and organized morning "walk-ins," during which they rallied together with parents and students alike. A February 2 text by Emily Comer paints the picture: "Our walk in was bad-ass. A ton of students. Lots of parents honked. Everyone was fired up, chanting, we even did the wave with our signs."

As the walkout approached, educators began collecting food donations to give to those large numbers of children who were dependent on school lunches and free breakfasts. Once the strikes began, teachers spent untold volunteering hours collecting and distributing food to these same students, often hand-delivering care packages to their homes.

A big strike is made up of many small acts of solidarity. One common highlight was the unexpected encouragement from parents. A large number of teachers recounted experiences similar to that of Tanya Asleson in Ravenswood, West Virginia:

On Wednesday [February 28] after the governor and union leaders reached that bad deal, I was out delivering food because I knew that day was particularly crucial: there was already open debates about going wildcat and I expected resistance from parents. I went to the house of a parent who was really poor, his kids always desperately need food at school. The strike was a real hardship for his family—but instead of telling me to go back to work, he said: "M'aam, you stay strong now. You haven't won yet, don't go back tomorrow." It was so moving.

One of the strikers' secrets to success was that they raised political demands—for example, massively increased school funding—that lie outside the restricted bounds of normal collective bargaining. The defense of student interests was put front and center. In Oklahoma, the work stoppage focused almost exclusively on demands for increased school funding, since the legislature had already passed important salary concessions in a last-minute attempt to prevent educators from walking out.

Fighting for students, and framing their struggles as a defense of essential services for the public, went a long ways towards undercutting the Right's constant harping that striking teachers were hurting children. Educators made a compelling case that they weren't walking from the students, but for them. As one West Virginia teacher explained in a March 1 letter to her students: "I love you and that's why I'm doing this."

Churches proved to be no less politically important for the red state revolt. Once the strikes began, a large number of church buildings became makeshift child care sites and food distribution centers. Many otherwise conservative pastors came out in favor of the teachers, which greatly consolidated the strikes' support base. Unlike in most union campaigns, this community alliance was not born from an agreement between labor leaders and relatively isolated progressive clergy. Instead, rank-and-filer workers and their family members directly brought the movement to their co-religionists. As one Arizona teacher explained on April 22, "I just talked to my 94-year-old mother who proudly told me that she had worn Red for Ed to church and to her women's group meeting and had talked to everyone she could about our cause. Oh, and we are also on the prayer list. #churchladieshaveourback."

Reversing Privatization

Burns is right to insist that rebuilding an effective fightback among public employees necessarily goes hand in hand with the project of reversing the privatization of public services. He puts it as follows:

> Just as conservatives have sought to reshape public policy by injecting their "free market" ideology into all realms of civil and economic society, labor must fight back by articulating the importance of the public sphere while delegitimizing the notion that the private sector is better or somehow more natural.

On this issue, there are some critical differences between the 2018 revolt and the last great round of rank-and-file radicalism in the U.S., the strike wave of the late 1960s and early 1970s described in *Strike Back*. Whereas the labor struggles of half a century ago came in the wake of a postwar economic boom and the inspiring successes of the civil rights movement, today's labor upheaval has erupted in a period of virtually uninterrupted working-class defeats and neoliberal austerity. As such, political scientist Corey Robin was right to call 2018's educator upsurge the "most profound and deepest attack on the basic assumptions of the contemporary governing order."[6]

The stakes are high. Public education remains one of the few remaining democratically distributed public goods in the United

States. For that very reason, corporate politicians have done everything they can to dismantle and privatize the school system. As Gordon Lafer documents in his book *The One Percent Solution*, this isn't only about immediate profit-making. Big corporations, he writes, are trying "to avoid a populist backlash" against neoliberalism "by lowering everybody's expectations of what we have a right to demand as citizens":

> When you think about what Americans think we have a right to, just by living here, it's really pretty little. Most people don't think you have a right to healthcare or a house. You don't necessarily have a right to food and water. But people think you have a right to have your kids get a decent education.[7]

As in the rest of the US, spending cuts have gone hand in hand with a push for privatization. The corporate playbook is not complicated. First, you starve public schools, then you insist that the only solution to the artificially created education crisis is "school choice"—i.e. privately run (but publicly funded) charters, as well as vouchers for private schools. In Oklahoma, there are now twenty-eight charter school districts and fifty-eight charter schools. "Is the government purposely neglecting our public schools to give an edge to private and charter schools?" asked Tulsa teacher Mickey Miller.

This nationwide offensive to take education out of the public sphere has undoubtedly advanced furthest in Arizona. About 17 percent of Arizonan students currently attend a charter school—more than three times the national average. Many of these schools generate millions of dollars in private revenue. Like many other parents in Arizona, Dawn Penich-Thacker questioned the state's priorities: "If there's so little funding for education, why should it be given to profit-making businesses?" In 2014–2015, for example, BASIS charter schools made almost $60 million for the private BASIS corporation that services its schools. "Business is business," noted Owen Kerr, who was formerly employed at BASIS. "So I can see that though a number of charters try to do things differently, most are set up to make money."

One of the major upshots of the red state revolt was that opposition to privatization has spread widely, particularly in Arizona. To quote Kerr, "this grassroots movement could very well be the first step towards reversing privatization in Arizona and beyond." Penich-Thacker explained how the state's Red For Ed movement had boosted anti-voucher sentiment in the state:

> Red for Ed has more people paying attention to education than ever before. Even last year, a lot of people hadn't heard of the funding crisis, let alone vouchers. Now you can't go anywhere in Arizona without talking about this. Red for Ed is an incredible "force multiplier" for efforts to put a stop to increased privatization: it makes all of our tools more powerful. Now every conversation we have about vouchers and charters is amplified across the state.

Though the initial pay and funding demands of these education movements may seem relatively modest, each walkout raised a question with radical political implications: Should our society's wealth and resources be used for human needs or corporate profits?

A small, but not insignificant, number of strikers concluded that systematic solutions will be needed to resolve our society's underlying crisis of priorities. When asked about her favorite moment of the strike, Morgantown teacher Anna Simmons recounted the following anecdote from the day West Virginian educators went wildcat:

> At a mostly unoccupied mall in Morgantown we met to discuss our options. Ultimately, in a nearly singular voice, we stated that we were not willing to accept the same empty promises our politicians have given their constituents for decades. It was a spontaneously planned meeting with short notice but our school employees showed up in huge numbers.
>
> I realized that night that I wasn't the only one feeling as passionately as I was feeling about what the work stoppage meant. It was the moment I realized that it was about more than just insurance premiums and salaries. It was the continuation of a movement that started with Bernie Sanders and is going to result in a power shift from the elite wealthy to the working people.

For readers interested in understanding the precedent for the 2018 education strikes—and in strategizing how to most effectively deepen their momentum across the U.S. in the coming period—*Strike Back* is an indispensable read. The book shows what tactics and strategies worked in the 1960s and 1970s and why these are essential to bring back today.

Burns also demonstrates that the fate of labor upsurges are not written in stone. It took hard work by organizers to make past labor victories possible. And, conversely, the decline of strike activity after the mid-1970s shows that militant workers and their unions must be ready to confront an intense pushback from employers and politicians. Both the carrot of Democratic Party co-optation and the stick of anti-strike repression should again be expected. Working people are up against powerful opponents.

Whether today's upsurge can continue to deepen, continue to spread, and continue to win remains to be seen. If history is any guide, the outcome of the current strike wave will be determined to a significant extent by the interventions of labor activists committed to workplace militancy and working-class independence. By arming themselves with the political lessons and history laid out in Joe Burns' *Strike Back*, public employees and union members across the country can effectively prepare themselves for the battles to come.

—**Eric Blanc, 2019**

INTRODUCTION

When the first edition of *Strike Back* was published in 2014, the attacks on public employee unionism were already well underway. Despite a massive grassroots mobilization by Wisconsin public workers in 2011, then Governor Scott Walker rammed through Act 10, which decimated public employee bargaining rights in the state. At the same time, several other states restricted public employee bargaining rights by limiting the subjects of bargaining or otherwise shifting the rules to favor employers.

Since 2014, these attacks have turned into an outright war against public employee unions, with a steady stream of state legislatures restricting bargaining rights. For example, in 2017, Iowa enacted legislation requiring union recertification votes prior to each bargaining cycle, eliminating dues checkoff. While, with tremendous expenditures of effort and resources, public employee unions won the recertification battle in Iowa, the legislation served to consume union resources and tilt the playing field dramatically in favor of employers. Other states have made it more difficult for unions to collect dues as well.

Since the election of Donald Trump in 2016, federal employee unions have been in a fight for their very existence, facing a virulently anti-union administration determined to overthrow decades of hard-won gains for public workers. Through executive orders, the administration has sought to kick union activists out of offices they have occupied for decades, eliminate lost time for union business, and overturn years of due process protections for federal workers. Although public employee unions have won some of the early court battles, there is no sign these attacks will abate.

In addition, privatization efforts have intensified in recent years, with teachers in particular facing relentless attacks through the charter school movement, which uses the guise of reform to destroy public education. The Trump administration is also trying to privatize the US Postal Service and threatening to do the same to the Veterans Health Administration, too.

And to top it all off, the most undemocratic institution in the United States, the unelected Supreme Court, has reversed decades of settled law, ruling in 2018 in *Janus v. American Federation of State, County, and Municipal Employees, Council 31* that public employees charging all members of their bargaining unit their full share of fees was unconstitutional.

While attacks are of course never something anyone wants, they do have a way of clarifying things. For public worker unions today, the issue has become quite simple: fight or die. Choosing the former, many public employee unions are increasingly adopting militancy in their attitudes and tactics. As we see in Eric Blanc's foreword to this book, a new generation of teacher activists are rising up and re-embracing the strike as a central part of their strategy. In the spring of 2018, West Virginia teachers fought back against years of underfunding of their schools, disrespect of their profession, and a system which condemned them to poverty for caring for their students. Their bold action, a statewide strike, captivated nationwide attention and pointed a way forward for the labor movement. Following on their heels, teachers in Oklahoma and Arizona also struck. These strikes in many ways mirrored the militant labor history described in this book. As is often the case, repression spawns resistance.

In many ways, today's public employee unionists are returning to their roots, looking back to a public worker union movement that was born out of militant, grassroots struggle in the 1960s and 1970s. Half a century ago, a strong, member-driven, aggressive labor movement stormed the halls of power. Public employees defied injunctions, often fought their very own international unions, confronted hostile politicians, as well as a corporate media out to destroy them. And they won.

While the focus of *Strike Back* is on public employees, private sector workers are also under attack and must figure out how to break free from an increasingly repressive system. They too need to study the militant history of public workers in the 1960s and 1970s, not just out of solidarity with their public employee brethren, but for their own survival.

Perhaps it's my background in bargaining for the last several decades, but I am full of hope. I believe the labor movement in this country will rise again, confronting power and privilege and ultimately providing a better way of life for millions of Americans. That is why the history of public workers in the 1960s and 1970s is so important—because it is a story of inspiration (and at times, strategy) for workers today.

1. THE STRIKE AND THE MAKING OF PUBLIC EMPLOYEE UNIONISM

Public workers are currently facing assaults on multiple fronts, including legislative attacks on their collective bargaining rights, bipartisan demands to gut hard won job protections and retirement benefits, and threats to privatize public services. In this hostile environment, understanding the incredible history of public employee militancy is a matter of survival for today's public sector unions.

The public employee strike wave of the 1960s and early 1970s provides historical evidence for the necessity of reviving the traditional, production-halting strike. In my previous book, *Reviving the Strike*, I argued that the contemporary labor movement needed to focus on redeveloping an effective strike. *Reviving the Strike* focused primarily on private sector unionism, using relatively few examples from the rich history of public employee unionism. This book aims to correct that imbalance, while also using the history of public employee unions as a jumping-off point to continue the larger discussion of how to regain union power. For a new generation of public employee unionists facing unprecedented attacks on their bargaining rights, learning this history is essential.

Prior to attending law school, I was the president of Local 1164 of the American Federation of State County and Municipal Employees (AFSCME). Even as an involved public employee trade union leader, I knew very little about the birth of the public employee union movement. While there were plenty of books on the struggles of private sector workers in the 1930s, not many materials covered the equally inspiring struggle of public workers in the 1960s and 1970s. For example, the official history of our union stressed the role of politicians in passing laws permitting collective bargaining, ignoring the story of the tremendous grassroots upsurge that was actually responsible for the rise of public employee unions. As Joseph McCartin, one of the few historians to extensively write about public employee strikes, points out, "[t]he explosive rise of public sector unions in the United States in the 1960s and early 1970s resembled in many ways the breakthrough of industrial unionism in the 1930s. … newly organized government workers behaved just as militantly as did auto and steel workers a generation earlier."[3] Today, as public employee unions face pressure on multiple fronts, the traditional methods of gaining influence—including lobbying and electing friendly politicians—have become less effective. That's why learning about the militant burst of collective action during the 1960s and 1970s is so important.

Finally, the story of the public employee upsurge of the 1960s and 1970s deserves to be told in its own right. Unfortunately, this history is currently mostly unwritten. As one professor complained, "I was at first surprised, and soon appalled, at the absence in virtually all survey textbooks, as well as in textbooks of the recent (post-1945) U.S., of any mention of the upsurge in public employee unionism in the 1960s and 1970s."[4] While much has been written about the other great protest movements of the era—the African American liberation struggle, the women's and anti-war movements—this inspiring bit of labor history has been largely neglected. Yet as Joseph McCartin explains, we should treat these public employee struggles as an important part of this period of protest:

> While the antiwar protests of 1970 are better remembered, the militancy of government workers was not less evident. New Jersey alone saw twenty-five public sector strikes—up from only one in 1962. During the first three months of 1970, U.S. public workers struck government agencies at a rate of one every thirty-six hours. Over a ten-week period, strikes erupted in twenty-four cities and twenty-eight schools systems.[5]

Public employees of the 1960s and 1970s faced many of the same issues that their counterparts do today. How to win bargaining rights in the face of repressive laws? How to build unionization in situations where formal recognition or majority support are not available or feasible? Should unions even have bargaining rights and the right to strike? How can unions win public support in the face of employer attempts to isolate them?

To many private sector workers, this list of challenges will sound familiar. Many of the topics addressed in this book—the relationship between labor law and strike activity, how to cope with injunctions, the right to strike—will be of interest to both public and private sector workers. After all, there are not two different labor movements in this country—a public and a private—

but only one, whose fates are inextricably woven together.

A Brief History of Public Sector Strikes

Public workers in the United States have a long history of strike activity, even though striking was illegal for public employees in every jurisdiction in this country until the late 1960s. According to the first comprehensive survey of public employee strikes, *One Thousand Strikes of Government Employees*, public workers struck 1,116 times from the mid-1800s through 1940 (571 of these strikes were against the depression-era Works Project Administration). While this is a mere fraction when compared to the approximately 300,000 private sector strikes in US history, this nevertheless demonstrates a longstanding desire among public workers to win a better life for themselves and their families through unionization.

One of the earliest public sector strikes occurred in 1835, when workers at the Navy Yard at Washington, DC "struck for a change in work hours and a general redress of grievances."[6] In all likelihood, those workers did not think of themselves as public employees on strike, but rather aggrieved workers looking to shorten the length of their workday to tolerable levels. According to labor historian Joseph Slater, "[d]istinctions between the public and private sectors were…more blurred in the nineteenth century than in the twentieth…Organized public employees were typically members of the predominantly private sector unions, such as skilled tradesman working in naval yards."[7]

Postal workers in the 1860s were the first group to attempt to form public employee-specific unions. However, their efforts were slowed when the postal service banned union membership in the 1890s, and President Theodore Roosevelt subsequently put in place a gag order preventing federal workers from lobbying for union membership. After agitation by the labor movement, Congress overturned Roosevelt's order with the Lloyd-La Follette Act of 1912, which allowed federal workers to join unions. The Act, however, failed to provide a mechanism for collective bargaining, hindering unionization efforts.[8]

It was during this time that public workers "began organizing more extensively as government employees."[9] As a result, public employee unionization levels rose dramatically, from less than 2 percent in 1905 to 3.5 percent in 1910, to 7.2 percent by 1921.[10] Much of this growth came during the great private sector union upsurge after World War I.

One of the most-discussed public worker strikes in US history occurred during this period—the 1919 Boston police strike. Like the 1981 air traffic controllers strike, the Boston police strike shaped public employee unionism for a generation. As a matter of fact, the issues at stake in the Boston police strike are still in play today. Writes Joseph Slater, "More broadly, the debate over the Boston Police Union turned on a central issue in American labor history: the extent to which government employees could be part of organized labor."[11] In the years preceding the strike, police around the country had begun to organize themselves into unions, submitting dozens of applications for charters to the American Federation of Labor (AFL). Worried about the strike actions of public workers, and ambivalent about accepting police officers as members given their traditional role in busting strikes, the AFL initially rejected the police applications. However, the 1919 AFL convention determined that "since police in various cities had organized and requested affiliation, the AFL would 'go on record as favoring' the organization of police unions and grant them charters."[12]

The complaints of the Boston police were "typical of all workers: low wages, long hours, unhealthy conditions and despotic supervisors."[13] The City of Boston, however, refused to recognize the police union or bargain for an agreement. After the union affiliated with the American Federation of Labor, the department fired numerous officers, targeting union leaders. At the time, government employees, and particularly police, could be fired for simply belonging to a labor organization, which was treated as a conflict of interest or disloyalty. In response to the firings and the failure of the police commissioner to address their concerns, on September 9, 1919, 1,100 Boston police officers walked off the job. The mayor took a hard line in response, and fired the striking workers. Massachusetts governor Calvin Coolidge, later to become President of the United States, sent in almost 5,000 National Guard troops to bust the strike. (In later years, the impact of the strike would be sensationalized, with reports of looting and vandalism.) Although many unionists in Boston pushed for a general strike in support of the officers, the leaders of the conservative Boston Central Labor Union backed away from this call, as they were "not ready to undertake what would have been one of the most daring and radical acts in the history of the AFL."[14] Ultimately, the police department refused to reinstate the striking police officers.

For public employee unionists of the era, the failure of the Boston police strike had the same chilling effect on unionism as Ronald Reagan's firing of striking air traffic controllers in 1981. "The aftermath of the Boston strike significantly restrained the movement for public sector unions," writes Joseph Slater. "All police locals affiliated with the AFL were soon destroyed."[15] Other public employee unions reacted by adopting no-strike clauses in their constitutions. As a consequence, the tremendous growth of public worker unions stalled, with the rate of unionization holding at barely eight percent throughout the 1920s.

In the years that followed, the failure of the Boston police strike was used to combat public employee unionism. As Joseph Slater summarizes, "Beyond the numbers, memories of the Boston strike inhibited the growth of public sector unions for decades; it became too easy to equate any form of public sector unionism with the calamitous confrontation."[16] Even today, opponents of public employee unionism still dredge up the Boston police strike. For example, conservative columnist Cal Thomas commenced a diatribe against the Chicago Teachers Union strike in 2012 by citing Coolidge's famous quote during the Boston police strike: "There is no right to strike against the public safety by anybody, anywhere, any time."[17]

From the 1920s through the 1950s, public employee unionism and strike levels continued to languish. As one scholar noted:

> Collective bargaining was not generally considered applicable to public employment until the late 1950s. The doctrine of state sovereignty, the domination of state legislatures by rural and anti-labor interests, unqualified acceptance of the prohibition against strikes by public employees, and the weakness of unions in public employment all contributed to the view that it was not a viable approach to improving the economic status of civil servants. The labor movement generally shared this view.[18]

Private sector unionization levels, however, skyrocketed during this time, as workers in key industries such as auto and steel forced employers to recognize their unions. Employing tactics such as mass picketing and sit-down strikes, private sector workers won major increases in real wages, employer-provided health care, and retirement plans. Public workers were for the most part left out of this upsurge, with public employee union density still stuck at 9 percent in the late 1950s. Part of the reason for this was that, until the late 1940s, "courts in all regions of the country imposed greater restrictions on unions in the public sector than on their counterparts in the private sector."[19]

That's not to say that public workers did not strike at all. Notable exceptions included teacher strikes over non-payment of wages during the Great Depression. However, these were short strikes over specific grievances, and did not result in union recognition. Most public employee strikes during the 1930s were concentrated among workers at the Work Projects Administration (WPA). From the start of the WPA in August 1935 through the end of 1937, "it did not have a single strike less month. In that period of two years and one-half it had at least 571 strikes."[20] WPA workers struck over a wide range of issues, including a living wage, establishing the union rate for skilled craft workers, and working conditions such as free transport to distant job locations. Strikers used a variety of tactics from picketing to takeovers of legislative meetings to sit-down strikes.[21] Inspirational as these examples were, they paled in comparison to the dramatic upsurge of private sector workers. Public employees for the most part sat out the strike wave of the 1930s. As a result, an entire generation of public workers missed out on the benefits of unionization.

The Beginnings of the Public Employee Upsurge

In the years immediately following World War II, a significant number of public workers struck as part of a massive strike wave of private sector workers. Many of the strikers were teachers, driven by "the post-war inflation" which was "creating a desperate situation for American teachers....The average pay for a teacher was $37 compared with $41 for a meat packer and $53 for a car worker."[22] As one study of teacher unionism noted, "during the war years, the average real income of industrial workers rose 80 percent while teachers' real income fell 20 percent. By 1945, the pent-up frustration of teachers burst forth in a brief but notable wave of strikes."[23] Despite opposition from their national organizations—both the American Federation of Teachers and the National Education Association opposed strikes—"there were successful strikes over pay in many communities," including Norwalk, Connecticut, Rankin, Pennsylvania, and Patterson, New Jersey. There were also significant strikes in St. Paul, Minnesota—with 1,160 teachers striking for over a month—and in Buffalo, New York, "where in February 1947, 2400 teachers walked out, closing eighty schools."[24]

Teachers were not the only group of public sector workers caught up in the excitement of the great post-World War II strike wave. In 1946, nearly 500 city workers in Rochester, New York "were fired for forming a chapter of the American Federation of State, County and Municipal Employees (AFSCME)." The city workers only got their jobs back when "30,000 private-sector workers quit work to rally in support of them in downtown Rochester."[25]

Legislators responded aggressively to these rumblings of public employee unionism, passing a flurry of anti-strike legislation "which explicitly covered public sector unions, but...were designed chiefly to provide draconian penalties for government workers who struck."[26] These laws were inspired by the burst of labor militancy in 1946, which " were a product of the era that produced the anti-union Taft Hartley Act."[27] For example, New York State's Condon-Wadlin Act, passed in response to the strike by teachers in Buffalo in 1947, required the automatic dismissal of any striker and required that any striking teacher who was rehired get no pay increases for three years and serve a five-year probationary period.[28]

As a result of these anti-public employee measures, the postwar strike wave soon subsided, and public worker strike activity remained low during the 1950s, with public employee unions favoring backroom deals over militancy. In addition, the Communist "red scares" of the era further dampened public employee militancy. At the same time, however, private sector unions were at the peak of their influence. Private sector workers struck repeatedly during the 1950s, averaging 350 strikes of over 1,000 workers per year during the decade.[29] In 1953, private sector union density peaked, with 35 percent of workers belonging to unions. In contrast, public workers rarely struck during this time, and when they did, their strikes were "illegal, small, and short."[30] In 1958, for example, there were only fifteen public employee strikes of any size in the entire nation.[31]

Lacking a strike or other mechanisms to resolve disputes, bargaining for public workers during the 1950s was little more than "collective begging." Unions lobbied government agencies for pay increases and were often unable to produce meaningful gains for their members. As Joseph Slater writes, "Absent statutes granting institutional rights, employers—mayors, school boards, and heads of departments—issued regulation that controlled labor relations. Not surprisingly, these policies were typically quite restrictive, often prohibiting affiliation with labor or organizing at all."[32]

The Public Employee Strike Wave

While the situation for public workers looked bleak at the conclusion of the 1950s, in reality, it was the calm before the storm. In a great strike wave that would span the next two decades, public workers across the nation would force obstructionist public employers to finally recognize their unions. Rejecting the backroom lobbying favored by the old guard, aggressive young public employee leaders demanded real collective bargaining, backed up by the right to strike. As a result of this surge, "Public sector strike activity increased dramatically during the 1960s and 1970s, despite the fact that such strikes were illegal in most states. Furthermore, public sector work stoppages increased to record levels at a time when strike activity was decreasing in the economy as a whole."[33]

Far and away the most militant group of public workers during this period were teachers. Teacher activism would reach its high point in the late 1970s, amounting to "nearly 44 percent of all work stoppages by local government employees during the 1974-1980 period . . . the largest percentage of work stoppages in public employment."[34] Following the example of teachers, sanitation workers, air traffic controllers, and social workers all embraced workplace militancy. From 1958 through 1970, the number of strikes of public workers "rose from 15 to 412 per year, workers involved from 1,720 to 333,500, and man-days of idleness as a result of strikes from 7,510 to 2,023,200."[35] This explosion of strike activity spanned the breath of the country, from major northern cities to rural western towns to southern "right to work" states.

Even police and firefighters joined in this workplace uprising. To take but one example out of many, police in the small Oregon community of Klamath Falls struck for union recognition in 1973. Entering the 1970s, the police officers of Klamath Falls were among the lowest paid in Oregon, received no overtime pay, and were often forced to work off the clock writing reports. When their department refused to bargain, eighteen police officers and clerks walked off the job on June 5, 1973. As a history of the strike noted, "although police strikes in Oregon were illegal, this was not to be the crucial issue. 'The big talk was not whether the strike was legal or not. It was a moral issue with the guys.'"[36] The city attempted to run the department with sergeants as both sides dug in for a long fight. The key breakthrough came when the sergeants, fed up with working twelve hour shifts during the strike, "complained they had lost their patience and would walk out if the strike was not settled soon."[37] The strike was ended shortly thereafter, earning the officers a ten percent pay increase. At the same time the police of Klamath Falls were striking, Oregon legislators were voting on passage of public employee bargaining legislation. The strike "served as a prime example of the type of dispute a comprehensive bargaining law was aimed at preventing."[38]

Rejecting the self-imposed prohibitions that had been in place since the 1919 strike in Boston, police began to strike across the nation, including in locations not considered union strongholds such as Oklahoma City, Tucson, and Las Cruces, New Mexico.[39] In October 1975, nearly 600 Oklahoma City police walked off the job, frustrated by the city's refusal to bargain. This was their third job action in eight years, which had included ticket writing slowdowns in 1967 and 1972. Fed up with years of inaction, administrator raises and poor supervisory practices, police again engaged in a ticket writing slowdown in 1975. This hit the city in the pocketbook, depriving it of revenue. An arbitrator then ruled that the police should be given large pay increases, but city officials refused to accept the ruling. (During this time, arbitrators would issue non-binding decisions which public officials often ignored if they did not agree with the ruling.) After city officials refused to abide by the decision of the arbitrator, outraged police officers began a campaign of radio silence, refusing to even acknowledge police calls. After an officer was rumored to be fired, the police began an impromptu march to city hall, with all on duty officers pulling their squad cars in front of the building. After one leader tossed his badge on the table at the city manager, "most of the department's 583 officers…filed into the meeting room and tossed their badges on the table as officers outside the building cheered."[40] Both sides were careful not to call the action a strike, which was settled after three days. Although the settlement included a 9 percent raise, it also included a penalty of two days for striking in addition to the three days lost pay during the strike. The city council at first refused to endorse the settlement, but threats by the police officers to initiate political recall petitions convinced enough council members to vote for the settlement, and the parties were soon able to establish a good bargaining relationship.

Firefighters also struck frequently during the 1970s. In Memphis, firefighters, upset that a purported $12 million city deficit had miraculously transformed into a $1.5 million surplus, struck for three days. After returning to work following an injunction, the firefighters walked out again after rejecting the proposed settlement, this time joining police on the picket line. After the involvement of the governor and the business community, the strike was settled in a compromise after eight days.[41]

Not all of the public employee strikes of this era were sanctioned by union leadership. In 1979, white collar state workers in New Jersey were represented by an independent union—the State Employees Association. After the SEA negotiated an agreement which failed to keep worker pay in line with the soaring inflation rate of the times, 15,000 New Jersey state workers responded with a wildcat strike.[42] Lined up against the striking workers was the state government, the courts, the media and their own employee association. Facing enormous pressure, the workers returned to work after three days, with no improvement in the state's position. The energy and solidarity developed on the picket line was not wasted, however. Dissatisfied with their union's response, the workers formed the State Workers Organizing Committee, which challenged the SEA in a state election. Affiliating with the Communication Workers of America (CWA), Committee organizers went on to win a representation election for 35,000 state workers in 1981. Building on the solidarity from the wildcat strike, the new union launched an aggressive contract campaign featuring informational picketing and grassroots mobilizing, backed up by a strike vote. With the 1979 wildcat strike fresh in management's memories, the first CWA contract secured "an unprecedented 17 percent across-the-board pay increase over two years," better healthcare, and greatly improved contract language.[43]

Factors Behind the Upsurge

A variety of factors contributed to the rise of public employee unionism during the 1960s and 1970s. First, there were profound changes in society, including a massive expansion of public employment. Labor historian Robert Shaffer writes about how "[t]he opportunity for public employee unions to arise was rooted in major postwar transformations in American life. These changes were at the core of a dramatic increase in overall public sector employment." Over a twenty-year period from 1946 to 1967, the number of public employees rose from 5.5 million to 11.6 million.[44]

This public employee upsurge was part of a larger movement for social change that took place during the 1960s, with the women's and civil rights movements in particular aggressively asserting their rights. These social movements helped infuse public employees with a hopeful attitude about change, with younger public workers, caught up in spirit of the times, bringing a culture of protest into the workplace. Labor arbitrator Arnold Zach, writing in 1972, noted that behind the growing public employee militancy was "a rising civil disobedience in the nation, as demonstrated in the civil rights movement, draft resistors' movement, anti-poverty activities and war protests, [which] convinced militant public employees that protest against 'the establishment' and its laws was fruitful and could be a valued vehicle for bringing about desired change."[45] This social unrest also provided natural allies for the rising public employee labor movement, a phenomenon which would be seen most clearly with the organization of sanitation workers in the South, who were able to strike and win collective bargaining agreements despite the anti-union attitudes prevalent in the region. Sanitation workers drew much of their strength from their allies in the civil rights movement. (As those movements waned and/or became institutionalized, sanitation strikes became less successful.)

In addition, since the private sector labor movement was far stronger than it is today, public employee unionists could point to other work groups such as unionized autoworkers or janitors who were receiving the benefits of collective bargaining. This not only fueled their demands, but made their arguments more credible to policymakers. Private sector unions also proved to be strong allies for striking public workers, with union labor councils pressuring public officials to settle disputes. Since private sector strike levels remained high during this period, public employee strikes reflected what was considered "normal" labor relations of the period.

All of these factors combined to create a favorable climate for public employee strikes during the 1960s and 1970s. Obviously, many of these conditions no longer exist. The modern private sector labor movement is on life support, barely able to sustain itself, let alone assist public employees under threat. Other social movements are similarly weak, with the great grassroots activism of the 1960s largely absent today. Despite all of this—or maybe because of it—the lessons of the militancy of the 1960s and 1970s are more important than ever for today's public employee unionists.

2. THE TEACHER REBELLION

In many ways, the public employee upsurge of the 1960s and 1970s began with the organizing efforts of a handful of teachers in New York City. Because of these committed educators, in the course of a decade, the United Federation of Teachers (UFT) went from being one of several tiny teacher organizations to a collective bargaining agent representing 55,000 members. This transformation was the direct result of repeated strike activity, which won collective bargaining rights, union representation and major improvements in pay and working conditions for teachers. By the power of example, these teachers in New York spurred a teacher rebellion that swept through the entire nation.

Entering the 1960s, teacher salaries lagged far behind those of other private sector workers in New York.[1] Things were so bad that a *New York Times* editorial asked why anyone would want to be a teacher when they could make more money working at a unionized car wash.[2] Teacher unions were also weak, with several competing organizations together only representing a fraction of the public school teachers in the city. Elementary school teachers formed the bulk of the UFT, while high school teachers belonged to a separate High School Teachers Association which focused on the divisive issue of establishing a pay differential between elementary and high school teachers.

Within the UFT, however, a movement was afoot in support of a strike-based strategy to improve the benefits and working conditions of teachers. This effort was led by a pair of tenacious organizers, each of whom would later go on to become president of the American Federation of Teachers, David Selden and Albert Shanker. Building from the ground up, Selden and Shanker spent most of the 1950s trying to gain support within the UFT for a strike. Their efforts finally paid off on November 7, 1960, when New York City teachers walked off the job in a system-wide one-day strike. While newspaper estimates concluded that only 5,600 of the city's 35,000 teachers had struck (a further 2,000 had called in sick), the fact that the organizers were able to even get 5,600 of their co-workers to strike was itself a major victory, as strikes by public employees were illegal in New York State and subject to harsh penalties under the Condon-Wadlin Act. [3] The one-day strike proved to be a smashing success, mainly because the organizers had scheduled the strike for maximum political effect—the day before Election Day. As a result of political pressure, and support from the then powerful labor movement in New York, the Board of Education agreed not to enforce the Condon Wadlin-Act, to hold a union election, and to establish collective bargaining for teachers. A year later, the UFT was overwhelmingly elected to represent teachers in New York City[4] The one-day strike not only spurred the organization of teachers in New York, but would become "the watershed for teachers' strikes in the twentieth century."[5]

The UFT went on to strike twice more over the next seven years, winning major improvements in the quality of work life for New York City teachers. In April 1962, half of the city's now

44,000 teachers joined the picket lines.[6] Through this strike, teachers won a thousand dollar across the board raise and free lunch periods. The next strike occurred in 1967, when 47,000 of the city's 59,000 teachers struck for two weeks. This strike earned teachers a 20 percent raise in pay and benefits, the right to have disruptive students removed from their classes, and additional funding to lower class size in schools identified as "high-need."[7] (In many of these early teacher strikes, contract demands included issues benefiting students, such as smaller class size.) As a result of their strike activity, by the early 1970s, teacher salaries had quadrupled. Labor historian John Lloyd notes how "[t]he significance of the early UFT strikes is difficult to overestimate, for the UFT had now set the standard for teacher contracts nationwide."[8]

The Teacher Strike Wave

Following the UFT's lead, teachers across the nation began to strike. From no reported strikes in the entire country in 1958, the number of teacher strikes soared to 112 in 1968.[9] Teacher strikes during that year ranged "from a strike in a one-teacher school in Maine to the massive state-wide strike conducted by Florida teachers of the NEA and the UFT strikes in New York City involving 57,000 teachers and excess of 1.1 million school children."[10] While the actual number of job actions constituted a small fraction of the nation's school districts, many of the strikes and threatened strikes were in large districts comprising thousands of teachers. Speaking about the strike wave, David Selden concluded that "it is no exaggeration to say that a clear majority of the nation's teachers were involved."[11] Even where teachers did not strike, they still took to the streets, packing school board meetings and protesting working conditions. As one account points out, "When not striking, teachers...carried their picket signs to city hall, held massive rallies and demonstrations, threatened to carry out mass resignations, and invoked what the NEA calls 'professional sanctions,' advising its members not to accept jobs in certain school systems."[12] This shift in membership activity was amazing. Whereas an average of only three districts per year saw strikes during the 1950s, by 1980, there were 232 teacher strikes nationwide.[13]

The era was ripe for a teacher rebellion. With industrial workers benefiting from sustained strike activity during the 1950s, teacher pay and benefits had fallen far behind that of other blue collar work groups. Additionally, at a time of massive expansion of the educational system, the profession was becoming increasingly bureaucratized, causing teachers to become "increasingly restive...regarding their lack of a greater voice in the determination of policies under which they work and what they consider as the economic neglect of schools in our affluent society."[14] As a result of their increasing militancy, teachers won unionization in city after city. By 1968, the AFT had become the collective bargaining agent for teachers in New York, Newark, Philadelphia, Boston, Washington DC, Chicago, Detroit, Cleveland, Kansas City, St. Louis, Toledo, New Orleans, and many other cities.[15] Teachers also struck in unlikely places, including a 1964 statewide strike in Utah and a one-day "professional study day" in Kentucky in 1966 "to protest the education budget passed by the State legislature."[16] John Chase, an organizer with the Washington Education Association, explained that the strike was the key weapon in winning these early teacher contracts: "When you create power, and the other side says no, you had to use your power!

We did not want to resolve conflict. We had to have confrontation....To take the strike out of the equation would have meant we would not have been a union."[17]

Through this intense upsurge of member-driven activism, teacher unions grew dramatically. By the late 1970s, over 70 percent of public school teachers were members of a union that represented them in collective bargaining, compared to less than a dozen school districts who could claim the same thing in 1961.[18] In little over a decade, teacher unions had gone from a negligible part of the labor movement to among its largest and most powerful organizations.

Teachers in Washington State Win Unionization Through the Strike

Although the Washington Education Association (WEA) had 34,000 members in 1964, the group's teachers "were not involved and in control of their organization." Instead, school administrators had disproportionate influence in WEA affairs, occupying positions of power within the union.[19] However, a new generation of teachers, influenced by the civil rights and anti-war movements, was demanding change. By the early 1970s, these militant teachers were "vying for control of WEA and its local associations ... [seeking] a stronger voice for classroom teachers in decisions vital to education and their own welfare."[20]

Although the Washington State legislature, at the prompting of the teacher's local in Seattle, had passed a public employee bargaining law in 1965, the statute had no mechanism to actually settle disputes. Understanding that the bargaining law had few teeth, school districts routinely ignored it. As a result, teachers became dissatisfied, and started pushing for greater control over their lives, "demanding to be equal partners at the bargaining table."[21]

By the early 1970s, with school districts stonewalling, WEA affiliates began to strike. Leading the way were not the big urban locals, as one might expect, but rather teachers in rural areas. On May 11, 1972, teachers in the small coastal community of Aberdeen, Washington staged the first strike of K-12 teachers in the history of the state. Although they went back to work after an injunction was issued, a blue ribbon panel was created in the wake of the strike, which granted the teachers many of their demands. Next, up was the Evergreen Education Association, outside of Vancouver, which would go on to win the first teacher collective bargaining agreement through striking in Washington State. In the fall of 1974, teacher strike activity continued with strikes in Federal Way, Tacoma, and Mukilteo.[22] In the face of this repeated illegal strike activity, legislators amended the state's collective bargaining law in 1975 to allow for, and regulate, strikes.[23]

Because of its militant actions, by the late 1970s, the Washington Education Association had established itself as a major force, and teachers in Washington State were now covered by strong collective bargaining agreements. The WEA, which had been dominated by school administrators in the early 1960s, had been transformed into a real union.

A Quarter Century of Strike Activity in Chicago

The experience of the Washington Education Association was replicated in state after state. One of the most militant groups of teachers of the era was the Chicago Teachers Union (CTU). Over a twenty-five year period from 1963 to 1987, the CTU repeatedly used the strike or the credible threat of a strike to gain collective bargaining rights, substantial pay increases, and to defend the public school system from harmful budget cuts.

In virtually every negotiation during this period, the CTU contract was settled only after a strike, or at the strike deadline. Ultimately, Chicago teachers became among the most highly paid in the country. Equally important, through their strike activity, the teachers improved public education in Chicago by reducing class size and preventing cuts to educational services.

For years the CTU, represented by longtime president John Fewkes, would make annual appeals to the Chicago Board of Education for collective bargaining rights, which the board routinely denied. The issues motivating teachers included low pay, safety in the classrooms, no duty free breaks, and lack of input into policy. As in New York, teachers in Chicago were divided between several competing organizations, including the local affiliate of the Illinois Education Association, which was not an advocate of collective bargaining. By 1963, Fewkes was able to use the teachers strike in New York as a bargaining chip during negotiations, telling the Chicago Board of Education that "[i]t is our desire that the board enter into good, fair negotiations without such strife as occurred in New York City."[24] Unlike in previous years, the union had something to back up its appeals for bargaining—the threat of a strike.

With the board continuing to deny the union's attempts at bargaining, the CTU began preparing for a strike in March 1964. On the eve of the mailing of strike ballots, however, the board of education reversed course and agreed to a collective bargaining memorandum.[25] One strike vote had accomplished what decades of begging and appeals to reason had failed to do. Unfortunately, the memorandum failed to provide for real collective bargaining or establish exclusive representation for teachers. Outraged, more militant teachers put pressure on Fewkes, denouncing the agreement as a "fake." The police had to be called when fifty members protested at a CTU meeting.

Ratcheting up the pressure, in each of the next three years, the CTU took strike votes and in each instance settled right at the strike deadline. In 1965, the strike threat won pay raises, and more importantly, an agreement to hold an election to determine which union would be the exclusive representative of Chicago teachers. In 1966, a strike was narrowly averted when the school board agreed to a $20 million settlement, including $500 pay increases and binding arbitration. In 1967, the CTU threatened to strike once again, settling only because of the mediation efforts of Mayor Richard Daley. Still, the union won a $1000 pay increase, ten paid vacation days, and more class room aides for elementary school teachers. A 1967 article in the *Chicago Tribune* concluded that the "strike gets results," and, commenting about the rising tide of teacher militancy in the greater Chicago area, added that:

> Teachers by the hundreds forsook textbooks for picket signs in the school year now ending in an unprecedented display of militancy to press for salary increases, collective bargaining rights, improved working conditions, and a share in making education policy. The Chicago area has been hit with nine teacher strikes since last November. Walkouts have been threatened in another dozen school districts.[26]

In 1968, Chicago finally saw its first teachers strike, although it was not officially sanctioned by the CTU. The core issue was the denial of full time status to a large group of primarily black teachers, who were also denied membership in the largely white local. With the expansion of enrollment, schools in Chicago had come to rely on what were called Full-Time Basis Substitute (FTB) teachers. These teachers—who were mostly African-American—worked full time, but lacked the benefits and job protections of regular teachers, and were not permitted full membership in the union. For years, the FTBs had fought for equality in their jobs and equal rights within the union. After a referendum to give them full membership within the union was rejected, the FTBs struck, without the approval of the union.[27] The strike impacted several hundred schools, lasting between two days and two weeks. While the strike did not produce immediate results for the FTBs, it did help build momentum for what happened the following year, when the CTU finally struck. That two-day strike won a $100 a month pay increase for teachers, and provisions improving public education, such as no cutbacks in summer school programs and class size limits. The strike also provided full certification for FTBs after three years on the job.[28]

Through strikes both real and threatened, the CTU was able to raise teacher salaries 90 percent between 1966 and 1974.[29] The union also gained substantial input into educational policy, paid vacation, group insurance, limitations on class size, and more preparation time for teachers. Over the next fifteen years, the CTU would strike eight more times. However, with the waning of the societal social movements of the 1960s and early 1970s, the bargaining climate became increasingly difficult. As a result, CTU strikes became longer and increasingly bitter, including a fifteen-day strike in 1983 and a month-long strike in 1986. By the mid-1980s, the CTU had come under more conservative leadership, and for the next twenty-five years abandoned the strike, until waging a high profile strike in 2012 against Mayor Rahm Emanuel's plan to gut public education.

Learning from Defeats

Even during the height of public employee unionism in the 1960s and 1970s, not every public worker strike ended in a resounding victory. No matter how supportive the environment, striking is never risk free, and American labor history is littered with the debris of failed strikes. Whether it was the great rail strikes of the late 1800s, the 1919 steel strike or the 1934 textile strike, striking workers have experienced their share of tough losses. That does not mean that these strikes weren't worthwhile, as successive generations often learned from, and built upon, the struggles of their predecessors.

One of the main lessons failed strikes taught public workers in the 1960s and 1970s was the necessity of community support. For example, most of the unsuccessful teacher strikes of the era occurred in rural, politically conservative areas without significant labor populations, where the striking public workers were isolated from supportive community forces. In 1969, 150 of the 430 school teachers in Minot, a small city in northwest North Dakota, struck over pay and working conditions.[30] Even after a state judge issued an injunction, the teachers continued to picket. In a case of unfortunate timing, a record flood hit Minot several days into the strike, pulling the public's attention and sympathy away from the teachers. However, the most damning element for the striking teachers was the political climate of the city of Minot. In the highly unionized urban areas of the northeast, striking teachers could rely on the support of unions and other progressive political groups. In conservative areas like Minot, politicians did not have to contend with such pressure and were free to take drastic measures against striking workers. In the end, the strike in Minot was defeated, and many teachers were fired.

Another failed teacher strike of the period that demonstrated the need for community support occurred in 1974, in the rural community of Hortonville, Wisconsin. Prior to the strike, the teachers in Hortonville had not received a raise for three years. The Hortonville School Board, however, refused to budge. Under Wisconsin state law at the time, a union had few options at the conclusion of negotiations; it could either accept the employer's final offer or be forced into an illegal strike. Choosing to fight, on March 19, 1974, eighty-four Hortonville teachers struck for a fair contract. It was a tough strike, featuring sheriffs escorting scabs through picket lines and the arrest of over seventy strike supporters. Taking a hard line, the Hortonville School Board fired all the striking teachers on April 1. The teachers attempted to rally support, and despite solidarity from teachers around Wisconsin, were unable to reverse the school board's decision. The union then tried to salvage the situation legally, but the courts proved to be of no help, although the issue of the firings went all the way to the US Supreme Court. In *Hortonville School District v. Hortonville Education Association*, the Supreme Court rejected the union argument that the firings violated the Due Process Clause of the Fourteenth Amendment to the Constitution.[31] The union argued that the school board should have given teachers individual hearings before depriving them of their jobs, but the Court brushed those concerns aside.

The strike was devastating to the teachers involved, with many forced to move out of state to find employment. Despite their defeat, the struggle of the teachers in Hortonville was not in vain. As the Wisconsin Educators Association Council notes on its website:

Every Wisconsin school employee is indebted to the Hortonville 84. Their firing heightened support among teachers for amending a bargaining law that forced teachers to strike illegally to achieve equity at the negotiating table. WEAC lobbying, along with nearly 50 other teacher strikes in the 1970s, and general unrest in teacher negotiations throughout the state, graphically revealed the flaws in the old bargaining law. The result was passage of a bill that legalized strikes and put in place a system of binding arbitration to resolve disputes.[32]

For today's public employee unionists, the lessons from defeats such as Hortonville and Minot should not be that striking is a mistake. After all, these defeats stand out more as exceptions rather than the rule. Nor should they read them to mean that public employees could not strike because strikes were illegal, as public workers successfully executed thousands of illegal strikes during this period. We also need to remember that although private sector workers supposedly have the "right to strike," many private sector strikes in the 1980s ended with workers out of jobs because they were permanently replaced after striking. Instead, the real lesson to be drawn from these failed strikes is that political context matters and that before striking, public workers must carefully assess their sources of support. In these strikes, public workers struck without sufficient support and suffered the consequences.

The War on Teacher Unionism

Today, teacher unionists find themselves under attack from multiple angles, including:

- Legislative efforts to change bargaining laws to limit their rights

- Attempts to limit or eliminate teacher pensions and tenure

- Efforts to privatize public education through the charter school system

- Attempts to deskill the teaching profession

- The Supreme Court's 2018 *Janus* decision, which ruled that union security provisions were unconstitutional

Taken together, these attacks are taking a toll on teacher unions. The National Education Association, the nation's largest teacher union, lost 230,000 members, or seven percent of its membership, from 2009 to 2013.[33] Since then, its membership numbers have remained essentially flat.

These anti-teacher efforts are spearheaded by well-funded conservative groups who hide behind progressive sounding rhetoric which masks their anti-union and anti-public worker agenda. Well-known intellectual Henry Giroux writes that

What is truly shocking about the current dismantling and disinvestment in public schooling is that those who advocate such changes are called the new educational reformers. They are not reformers at all. In fact, they are reactionaries and financial mercenaries who are turning teaching into the practice of conformity and creating curricula driven by an anti-intellectual obsession with student test scores, while simultaneously turning students into compliant subjects, increasingly unable to think critically about themselves and their relationship to the larger world.[34]

The underlying philosophy of these "reformers" is based on right-wing economic theory. As commentators Doug Henwood and Liz Featherstone note, "[t]o charter-school boosters, education should be restructured to resemble the free market of economic theory, in which sellers of school product compete for the custom of parents."[35]

None of this is to say that the educational system does not face severe problems, including urban school districts that have been hit hard by de-industrialization, continued racial segregation of housing and labor markets, and declining tax bases. Yet, as education activist Lois Werner states, these so-called reformers "presume that if children do not succeed at school, the responsibility rests solely with the school. Such an approach destroys the structure and organization of a publicly-funded and presumably publicly-controlled system of education begun more than a century ago."[36]

Rather than fight back, the predominant response of many teacher unions has been to attempt to appear reasonable and "negotiate for change." The problem with this strategy of cooperation is that there is little reason to believe that corporate education reformers are actually looking to improve public education. Instead, their real goal is to privatize the educational system, remove the autonomy of classroom teachers, and most importantly, get rid of unions.

For these reasons, teacher unions need to rediscover the lessons of their own history. Fifty years ago, teachers raised concerns over lack of professional autonomy and input into educational decisions, responding to attacks on their profession with an outpouring of militancy that established collective bargaining and "changed the fundamental relationship between teachers and administrators. It promised teacher more say in the conduct of their work, more pay and greater job security. It essentially refined and broadened the concept of professionalism for teachers by assuring them more autonomy and less supervisory control."[37]

As Eric Blanc explains in his introduction to this book, in many ways, the 2018 teacher strike wave in states such as Arizona, Oklahoma and West Virginia harkens back to the militantism of a half century ago. The defying of injunctions, the strong social unionist message, the effectiveness of strategic strike activity, and the incredible grassroot nature of the "red state rebellion" all appear to be lifted out of the pages of history.

3. THE BACKLASH AGAINST PUBLIC EMPLOYEE UNIONISM AND THE DECLINE OF THE STRIKE

As the US economy sputtered in the post-Watergate era, a backlash developed against public employee unions. With workers continuing to press wage demands and strike repeatedly while the economy suffered, unionized employees began being painted as overpaid and taking advantage of taxpayers.

In this anti-union climate, politicians from both sides of the aisle realized that political gain could be had by getting tough on public employee unions. Joseph McCartin explains that "[b]y the mid-1970s, government officials at all levels dealt with the growing fiscal crisis through budget cutbacks, hiring freezes, and hardline union negotiations. As often as not, the austerity programs were instituted by Democratic administrations once allied to the public sector union movement."[1] Pollster Louis Harris told the US Conference of Mayors in 1975 "that the way to get elected was to get tough on public workers."[2] Some mayors even tried to goad public workers into striking in order to create fights with unions they were now confident they could win. For example, the mayor of Utica, New York complained to *Business Week* in 1975 that "I can't get anyone to go on strike against me.

I think city government needs a showdown with the unions."[3]

This shift in the bargaining climate is best demonstrated by the changing fortunes of sanitation workers in the South. During the 1960s, the struggles of southern sanitation workers were embraced by the civil rights movement. In cities such as Memphis and Charleston, civil rights leaders were arrested on the picket lines while supporting striking workers. Even as late as 1970, when the white mayor of Atlanta threatened to replace striking sanitation workers, civil rights organizations lined up to oppose the move.[4] With the civil rights movement still strong, and the memory of urban rebellion fresh in the minds of local officials, compromise was the preferred method of settling disputes. Joseph McCartin writes about how the sanitation strikes that erupted between 1968 and 1972 in cities such as Cleveland, Miami, Washington DC, Lubbock, Texas and Atlanta "were typical of a new pattern of municipal labor-management conflict... During each of these strikes, officials had the power to replace striking sanitation workers. Yet in each case officials either decided not to use this tactic or, after attempting to replace strikers, dropped the effort under pressure."[5]

By the mid-1970s, however, with the country facing a fiscal crisis, "'standing up to' public sector unions became the litmus test of a politician's sense of fiscal responsibility." This was particularly true for Democratic politicians, "who had to fight the charge that they would 'give away the store' to their labor allies."[6] As an example, former civil rights activist Maynard Jackson had been elected Atlanta's first black mayor in 1973. Facing reelection in 1977, Jackson wanted to win over middle class whites and the business community. Like many cities during this period, Atlanta faced a budget shortfall. When primarily black sanitation workers struck on March 28, 1977, Jackson took a tough stand, firing the workers and declaring the strike over. Jackson then began hiring replacement workers, rebuffing an offer by the union to end the strike if the fired workers could get their jobs back. Unlike in previous strikes, the major organizations in the African-American community lined up against the striking workers. Isolated from allies in the civil rights movement, and with no strong labor support behind them, the union surrendered and ended the strike. While most of the striking workers managed to get their jobs back at their old rate of pay, the union had been dealt a crushing defeat.[7]

Following the failure of the sanitation strike in Atlanta, other Democratic mayors followed suit, with striking sanitation workers fired in San Antonio, Texas and Tuscaloosa, Alabama. Even Detroit Mayor Coleman Young, a former union organizer in a union stronghold city, threatened to fire striking sanitation workers if they did not end a wildcat strike.[8] After workers represented by AFSCME struck in August 1978 despite a court injunction, Young ordered city officials to draw up termination papers for the 3,500 employees. Under the threat of losing their jobs, the striking workers relented and ended their walkout. Half a decade before Ronald Reagan fired air traffic controllers in a move that put the government's stamp on union-busting, Democratic mayors were already firing public employees for striking.

Union Busting and the PATCO Strike

In 1981, President Ronald Reagan famously fired over 11,000 members of the Professional Air Traffic Controllers Organization (PATCO) for conducting an illegal strike. This action initiated a tougher approach to public employee strikes by the federal government, and helped dampen strike enthusiasm among public sector workers in the decades to come.

The experience of PATCO from the mid-1960s through the 1981 strike in many ways tracks the trajectory of the public employee labor movement. The union traces its origins to employee efforts in the aftermath of a December 1960 midair aircraft collision over Brooklyn, New York that killed 134 people. Concerned that the Federal Aviation Authority (FAA) was deflecting blame from fundamental problems with the nation's air traffic system, the controllers began networking and organizing. Initially turning to a federal employee union, the National Association of Government Employees, in the mid-1960s the controllers took a more militant turn and began looking to form their own organization. Aided by legendary trial lawyer F. Lee Bailey, the controllers formed PATCO in 1968.

At the core of PATCO's formation were militant job actions, including slowdowns and sickouts. Joseph McCartin writes that, "Between 1972 and 1977, PATCO emerged as the most militant, most densely organized union in any bargaining unit of the nation's largest employer, the U.S. government."[9] In 1968, the union engaged in a slowdown dubbed "Operation Air Safety." The following year, frustrated by the FAA's refusal to follow through on commitments made in the wake of the slowdown, the controllers conducted a sickout. In response, the FAA cracked down on the union, cancelling dues check off and leaves of absences for union officials and engaging in retaliatory transfers. Choosing to fight rather than back down, one-quarter of the nation's air traffic controllers participated in a strike in the spring of 1970, thinly disguised as a sickout. Despite incredible pressure, including threats of termination, lack of support from the pilot's union, and injunctions, the strikers held out for nineteen days. The strike did not end well, with the firing of eighty controllers and none of the union's demands met (the workers were later rehired in a deal with President Richard Nixon).

Despite this setback, PATCO rebounded and managed to negotiate its first collective bargaining agreement in 1973. This contract was in many ways the high water mark for PATCO, as bargaining became increasingly difficult as the 1970s wore on, which was the case for most public employee unions. By late in the decade, the union was increasingly bumping heads with the Carter administration, which had been taking provocative action against the controllers, including canceling an early retirement program, rescinding a safety immunity program, and refusing to address pay, which was the number one issue for the union membership.[10] Frustrated and angered by the government's actions, support for a strike began building within the organization.

During the negotiations for a new contract, Ronald Reagan took office in January 1981. By threatening to strike, PATCO was able to reach an agreement with Reagan, "winning approval from a conservative president for a contract that far exceeded anything the federal government had offered a union before."[11] Although federal law does not permit negotiations over wages, PATCO was able to secure a pay increase, night differential and other improvements. The level of hostility against the government was too high among union members, however, and the contract was rejected by 95 percent of the membership. Even though the settlement contained impressive gains, opponents focused on the failure to win some of the more ambitious demands, such as a thirty-two hour work week.

On August 3, 1981, PATCO workers began the first officially

sanctioned national strike against the federal government. Previous federal worker strikes had been local affairs or wildcat actions, such as the 1970 postal strike, which had not been supported by the national union leadership. The PACTO strike, in contrast, was an undisguised strike called by the national union which directly challenged the authority of the federal government. Unfortunately, PATCO leaders failed to understand that the ground was shifting beneath their feet, with an increasingly vocal conservative movement declaring war on public employee unions. In fact, many conservative organizations complained that Reagan had gone too far by agreeing to the terms of the rejected PATCO contract in the first place. Drawing a line in the sand, the president set a deadline for the strike to end, and when the striking PATCO workers failed to meet that deadline, he fired over 11,000 air traffic controllers.

Today, many point to the PATCO strike as the root cause of the employer offensive against workers in the 1980s. This is not accurate. While the PATCO strike greatly contributed to the union-busting atmosphere, management's war against labor was going to happen regardless, as employers had become increasingly aggressive in the late 1970s against both private and public sector workers. The falling rate of corporate profits, pro-management labor law, and the growth of right-wing ideology all developed independent of the PATCO strike. The firing of the PATCO strikers was a dramatic indicator of the new terrain, rather than the creation of it.

Cooperation Instead of Confrontation

As the bargaining climate continued to worsen for public workers in the 1980s, many public employee unionists decided that a policy of cooperation was the best way to move forward. With most public employee unions now favoring participation in electoral politics and behind the scenes lobbying over the confrontational tactics of the previous two decades, public employee strike levels dropped dramatically.

Public sector strike activity reached its peak in 1979, with 593 strikes nationwide. Those levels quickly plunged, however, dropping to a mere seven strikes in 1982.[12] In sharp contrast to the hundreds of public employee strikes during the 1970s, from 1988 to 1998 there were an average of only 6.5 public employee strikes per year.[13] None of this is to say that the strike completely disappeared during this period. State workers struck in Minnesota in 1981 and 2001. Transit workers continued to strike, in Los Angeles, Minneapolis, New York, Philadelphia, and San Francisco, among other cities. Although at lower levels, teachers continued to strike in states such as Pennsylvania and Vermont. However, for the most part, the confrontational tactics of the 1960s and 1970s were over.

In addition to unions' newly found belief in cooperation over confrontation, there are several other reasons for the decline of public employee strike activity in the 1980s and 1990s. First, the decline of public worker strikes tracked the overall decline of strikes in the private sector. Historically, public employee strike levels have been highest when other workers were striking as well. During the 1980s, private sector strike activity plummeted. Second, a more aggressive employer response made many unions think twice about striking, with President Ronald Reagan's firing of PATCO workers the most well-known example of this new hardline approach. Finally, in response to the illegal strike wave of the 1960s and 1970s, laws in many states improved the collective bargaining process. As a result, as of 2011, thirty-one states provided some form of interest arbitration for public workers.[14] Under interest arbitration, a neutral arbitrator makes the final decision of what is included in a contract. By providing a mechanism to settle contracts, interest arbitration reduced strike levels.

Furthermore, in response to the strike wave of the 1960s and 1970s, many states passed laws regulating bargaining by public workers. By 1999, thirty-four states had laws on the books providing for collective bargaining, while another six states authorized some form of representation.[15] These laws varied widely in terms of which workers were covered, the subjects of bargaining that were permitted, and whether or not workers could strike or utilize binding arbitration. In general though, these laws helped regularize labor relations in the public sector. Whereas in the early days of collective bargaining, unions were free to bring forward matters of policy and issues of concern to the community such as classroom size, under the new framework, bargaining was often restricted to wages and other narrow working conditions. In addition, unlike the heady days of the 1960s and 1970s, negotiations were often conducted behind closed doors with little membership participation. Bargaining became routine, and many unions embraced the concept of labor-management cooperation.

This seeming stability, however, masked increasing problems for public sector workers. Just as a segment of the right-wing never accepted bargaining in the private sector and worked for decades to gut the right to strike, similar opposition focused on undermining public sector bargaining. Spurred by libertarian law professor Sylvester Pestro and his anti-public employee Public Service Research Council, these anti-public employee union organizers merged with the tax revolt movement to help propel Ronald Reagan into office in 1980.[16] Bashing public employee unions was very much part of their message.

This ascendant conservative movement attracted the support of powerful funders who over the course of the next two decades built up a network of right-wing foundations and think tanks. Years before he was propelled onto the national scene during the upsurge in Wisconsin, far-right billionaire David Koch was funding and building his own conservative empire. The son of one of the founders of the far right-wing John Birch Society, Koch ran for vice president in 1980 on the Libertarian Party ticket. Over the next two decades, he would help create a web of right-wing organizations which increasingly targeted public employees.

By and large, public employee unions attempted to temper this conservative onslaught by moderating their demands and avoiding confrontation. Initially, this strategy of lying low and engaging in politics produced acceptable results, as public employee unions for the most missed the vicious anti-employer assault of the 1980s and 1990s. While the percentage of private sector workers covered by collective bargaining agreements dropped from 23.3 percent in 1977 to 7.3 percent in 2012, public employee levels remained fairly constant during the period, dropping only from 40.1 percent to 39.6 percent.[18] And while most private sector unions have lost defined benefit pension plans and seen increased healthcare costs, public sector unions have largely maintained better retirement and healthcare benefits.

However, this period of seeming stability for public sector unions was, in reality, the calm before the storm. In 2003, Richard Hurd of Cornell University perceptively sounded the alarm in a series of articles about the coming crisis of public employee unionism, arguing that it would be a mistake "to conclude that public sector unions are strong, stable, and immune to the external and internal influences that have brought private sector unions to their knees."[19] In the decade and a half since the publication of these articles, Hurd has proven to be correct and then some, as public sector unions have faced an all-out assault on multiple fronts, including attacks on their collective bargaining rights, wages and pensions.

The Future of Public Employee Militancy

In one of the first of many conservative salvos against them, Indiana public employees lost collective bargaining rights in 2006. "We have a new privileged class in America,' said Indiana's then Governor, Mitch Daniels, upon rescinding the workers' collective bargaining power on his first day in office. "We used to think of government workers as underpaid public servants. Now they are better paid than the people who pay their salaries."[20]

In the years since then, the war against public employee unions has only escalated. Despite the protests of tens of thousands of Badger State residents, Wisconsin Governor Scott Walker signed a restrictive public employee bargaining law in 2011, eliminating bargaining rights for several groups of public workers, barring interest arbitration, limiting bargaining to wages, limiting dues collection, and requiring union recertification. Michigan also passed a controversial law allowing emergency managers to be appointed and other statutes barring union dues collection and limiting the subjects of bargaining for school employees. Bargaining rights were also weakened in Idaho, Nevada, New Jersey, Oklahoma, and Tennessee. On the federal level, the Trump administration has issued executive orders rescinding union rights and has imposed collective bargaining agreements on unions.[21]

While some Democratic states, following the Supreme Court decision in *Janus*, have passed legislation protective of public employee bargaining rights, conservative groups have shown no indication of letting up the pressure, with numerous cases currently winding through the courts challenging public employee bargaining.[22]

Public workers are thus being compelled to fight against forces who want not only to destroy their unions, but to dismantle the public sector itself. The severity and coordinated nature of these attacks make it clear that cooperation is no longer an option. All of this has been a wake-up call for public employee unions, who are finally beginning to understand that their strength comes from a mobilized membership. As politicians attempt to turn the clock back to a time when public workers had no legal bargaining rights, public employee unionists must also reach back in time to learn the lessons of their militant predecessors.

4. PUBLIC EMPLOYEE SOCIAL UNIONISM

Public and private sector strikes involve two very different types of strategies. While the aim of the private sector strike is to "exert economic pressure on the employer by depriving him of revenues," the purpose of the public employee strike "is to exert political pressure on municipal officials," so that "they are deprived, not of revenues but of the political support of those who are inconvenienced by a disruption of municipal services."[1] In short, the private sector strike attempts to affect the employer economically, while the goal of the public sector strike is primarily political.[2]

As a matter of fact, public employers typically save money during public employee strikes by continuing to collect taxes and other revenues that they would have normally paid to the striking workers. Take the example of a strike by librarians at a county library. The county would save money during the strike because even though the library is closed, the county continues to collect the same amount of tax revenue, but does not have to pay wages. The strike would end only when enough members of the community demanded the restoration of library services. Similarly, if workers struck the state Department of Motor Vehicles, the employer—the state—would stop paying the striking employees. The pressure to settle the strike would come not from lost revenue, but from the outcry of citizens who could not get their licenses renewed, switch titles, etc. Unlike in the private sector, "loss of revenue does not motivate a public employer to settle a strike." Instead, the goal of the union "is to make the strike's interruption of government services of sufficient political cost to motivate the employer to settle on more favorable terms."[3]

On a broader level, public employee strikes involve questions of the public good and social and economic policy, such as the education of children, the provision of social services, and the imposition of taxes. Accoring to Paul Johnston, author of *Success While Others Fail,* a study of public employee social unionism, public employee unions "are involved in public issues: because they confront them face-to-face—at the point of production, so to speak, of society itself; because their fate is closely linked to the status, funding and fate of their employing agencies."[4] The goal of a teachers strike, for example, is not just to shut down the school, but to pressure policymakers to adopt a different stance towards issues such as school funding which have become intertwined with immediate contract demands. As a result, community ties, political influence and message framing are critical in public employee strikes. Protest and disruption matter to the extent that they impact those with resources in the community. A teacher's strike which inconveniences working parents generates a different level of political heat than a strike in a state agency that has little contact with the public. The leverage of public sector workers varies based on the political support they are able to obtain for their cause. The more a strike can limit operations, the greater the impact on the public, which in turn leads to more pressure on municipal officials to settle.

Since the primary aim of a public employee strike is to put

pressure on policymakers, the tactics that the union engages in are very important. These strategy concerns pop up in very practical questions. For example, if you are a union at a public university, do you strike on the first day of class when you can have the biggest impact on operations, or later in the semester, when you have more time to build political support? Do you picket every door or focus on more impactful public areas? Do you conduct a one-day strike or an open-ended one? The strategy that is ultimately chosen should be the one that will mobilize the community, garner publicity, and pressure public officials. However, this may not always be the strategy that impacts services most directly.

Finally, unlike in the private sector, the services provided by public workers are not paid from profit produced during the production process. Typically, public employee wages are paid for by taxes. For this reason, contract settlements frequently veer into discussions of taxation and government policy, providing an opportunity for anti-labor forces to politicize the issues. There are exceptions to this trend, as some public employees work in jobs which partially rely on revenues to succeed. For instance, if workers at a county hospital go on strike, the hospital could lose patient revenue, making the dynamics similar to that of a private sector strike. But even here, because public hospitals are typically subsidized by government agencies and tend to provide services to poor communities, the strike would still have a political dimension.

Ultimately, if a public employee union attempts to conduct a strike like its private sector counterparts, it will likely lose. Instead, the task is to combine the community support of social unionism with the workplace-based nature and power of the strike. In true social unionism, workers forge deep ties to the greater community.

"Economic actions but as political mobilizations"

In the aforementioned *Success While Others Fail*, Paul Johnston draws on his experience as an organizer of public employee unions in San Francisco and San Jose to argue for a form of public employee unionism with strong community ties. Throughout the 1970s, public employee unions in San Francisco engaged in high levels of strike activity. Many of these strikes were straightforward affairs lacking any effort to frame the issues or reach out to the community. At their worst, these strikes were narrow economic actions, oblivious to public perception. During the height of public employee power in the early 1970s, unionists could get away with purely economic strikes. By the late 1970s, however, public employee unions had begun to come under attack from conservative forces within government and society. Joseph McCartin writes about how

> The volatile recipe of rising public sector union militancy, inflation, and anti-tax activism made public sector unions more vulnerable than they had been at any time since the rise of their movement in the 1960s. Suddenly, the union became a convenient political scapegoat for public officials who had to deal with declining relative tax revenues, demands for improved public services, and taxpayer unrest.[5]

This new and aggressive anti-public employee union attitude took hold in San Francisco. After the assassination of Harvey Milk and Mayor George Moscone in 1978, a new breed of conservative San Francisco Democrat—epitomized by politicians such as Dianne Feinstein—realized that they "could direct blame for the fiscal crisis, tax increases, and urban social problems away from public officials and corporate power and toward public workers and their unions."[6] Public employers in the city came to understand the importance of framing their arguments against public workers, seizing on issues such as an alleged $17,000 street sweeper as a symbol of overpaid public employees.[7] To the extent that union bargaining demands and strikes became just about increased wages for public workers, management began to win the battle for public support. In addition, high profile missteps— such as when raw sewage spilled into San Francisco Bay during a union strike—harmed the image of public workers.[8]

In response, progressive California public employee trade unionists developed what Johnston calls "public employee social unionism." These unionists realized that the issues "they emphasized and the manner in which they framed them were of central importance, in part because they saw how politicians skillfully used issues against them."[9] They also understood that they needed to have community support, and to strike over issues of broad public concern. For instance, rather than striking over higher wages, a teachers union would strike over the quality of education. In contrast to many failed or marginally successful public strikes of the mid to late 1970s, unions were more successful when they reached out to the community and framed their issues not as "economic actions but as political mobilizations."[10]

One example of this new strategy was a strike by workers at the San Francisco Public Housing Agency in November 1978. Facing newly elected Mayor Dianne Feinstein, who was attempting to make a name for herself by taking on public workers, the union needed to adopt new tactics. Prior to the strike, the union established ties with tenants groups by focusing on the issue of mismanagement. Johnston writes how

> Although the strikers made several demands, from higher wages to improved health and safety at work in the projects, they emphasized one issue: mismanagement. They labeled the housing authority 'the worst slumlord in San Francisco' and demanded a voice in its reform. They accused their employer of incompetence and of being unable to carry out the agency's mission. They defined their strike, in other words, as a campaign for safe and decent housing in San Francisco's decaying, crime infested projects.[11]

Building on the relationship the union had made prior to the strike, the tenants' association joined the battle, engaging in a rent strike with a "set of demands for better security in the projects." The participation of the tenants' association "added the political weight of some twenty thousand tenants to that of the few hundred housing authority workers already on strike."[12] As a result of this dual pressure, the city quickly settled with the striking workers.

However, when the union committee presented the settlement to a packed room of striking workers, a member asked if the tenants' association had reached a settlement, too. The membership was then told that the city had refused to meet the tenants' demands. Instead of accepting the settlement, the union unanimously voted to remain on strike until the tenants' demands were satisfied. After two days, the housing authority reached an agreement with the tenants' association and the strike ende. By fighting together, the union and the tenants' association were able to strengthen each other's struggles and emerge victorious, in a wonderful example of social unionism.

Another example of true social unionism involved the Social Service Employees Union (SSEU) which represented "social investigator, home health care aides and counselors in New York City's Department of Welfare."[13] Leading up to a strike in 1965, SSEU activists built alliances with an emerging movement of welfare recipients. When the city "attempted to cast the welfare strike as an attack on clients," the welfare recipients joined the SSEU workers on the picket lines. The union, in turn, asked that the demands of the welfare clients be incorporated into their contract demands. Two days into the strike, the city dismissed 5,398 Welfare Department workers for striking in violation of state law.[14] The workers ignored the action as well as a state court injunction and remained on strike despite the jailing of nineteen strike leaders.[15] During the strike, SSEU members were also joined on the picket lines by clerical workers in the Department of Welfare represented by AFSCME Local 371.

The strike was settled after twenty-eight days, with an agreement that set up a fact finding commission, dropped jail sentences against strike leaders, and provided amnesty for striking workers. The contract agreement that was subsequently reached included a 9.44 to 11.57 percent pay increase, case load limitations, and health care improvements. Notably, the settlement included an automatic clothing grant for welfare recipients, a subject city officials had vigorously contended was management's sole purview and not a proper subject of collective bargaining. (It took the threat of a sit-in to force Mayor Robert Wagner to sign the contract.)[16] Crucial to the victory was "widespread democratic decision making and a commitment to participation by members," support from welfare rights leaders, and the solidarity from AFSCME Local 371.[17]

This incredible unity, however, was short-lived. When the SSEU contract with New York City expired in 1967, the union engaged in an unsuccessful three-day strike that was not supported by Local 371.[18] After several months of post-strike fact finding failed to produce an agreement, SSEU responded with a "work-in" where employees would report to work, but not perform any tasks.[19] The union was ultimately forced to submit their dispute to mediation, and many of the groundbreaking provisions such as the clothing allowance were lost.

The difference in outcome between the 1965 and 1967 strikes can in part be explained by a change in employer attitude. Freaked out by the small but feisty SSEU, the city shifted its strategy to begin favoring larger more established unions such as AFSCME. While "union democracy and the presence of organized socialist militants were the primary reason for the 1965 alliance with welfare rights groups," opposition from the city "in the form of a major enforced institutional change blocked such an alliance from effectively continuing past 1967."[20]

Teacher Unionism and the Civil Rights Struggle

Some of the best examples of social unionism occurred during the 1960s, when public employees joined with the civil rights movement, linking trade unionists and African-Americans together in shared struggle.

Perhaps the most famous of these joint civil rights/labor fights was the 1968 Memphis sanitation workers' strike. The Memphis strike was part of a larger wave of public worker strikes during this time, many of them in the South. As one analysis noted at the time, "[s]trikes in the South have the dubious distinction of being second only to those in the Northeast when it comes to the intensity of strike activity."[21]

While the Memphis sanitation strike has gone down in history mainly because of the assassination of Martin Luther King, Jr., many other lesser known struggles of the time are just as important to the history of public employee social unionism. For example, in March 1969, hospital workers in Charleston, South Carolina struck for pay equity and union recognition. After local authorities arrested over 100 striking workers, the dispute became a major civil rights battle, with the Reverend Ralph Abernathy—who succeeded Dr. Martin Luther King Jr. as President of the Southern Christian Leadership Council—assuming leadership of the effort.[22] The strike was finally settled after months of civil disobedience—Reverend Abernathy was jailed at one point for inciting a riot—and turmoil in the city.[23] Today, many in the labor movement consider southern "right to work" states virtually impossible to organize. Yet, as the strikes in Memphis and Charleston indicate, in the 1960s, public workers in the South were able to successfully obtain collective bargaining rights.

As much as these struggles revealed the power of a unified labor and civil rights movement, a set of labor conflicts during the same time period demonstrated the exact opposite. In the late 1960s, teacher unionists collided with the African-American community in a heated battle in New York City. In 1967, as part of an experiment in community control prompted by a sit-in at the Board of Education, a local board in the Brownsville neighborhood of Brooklyn was given greater control over its school district. Soon, community board members in the primarily

African-American neighborhood "claimed sweeping powers in the district, including the sole right to determine curriculum, control expenditures, and hire and fire personnel."[24] Coming out of the Black Power movement, these activists argued that the largely white teaching force could not properly educate students in their overwhelmingly African-American neighborhood. As a result, community members sought control over their schools, including the right to transfer or fire white teachers.

After the community board refused to let white teachers report to work, the United Federation of Teachers called for a strike in the district. An increasingly conservative and combative Albert Shanker, head of the union, attacked the community groups, claiming they were anti-Semitic. Shanker also ostracized African-American unionists who attempted to find a middle ground between the two parties. Ignoring the racial component, for Shanker, the dispute was over basic union rights, such as the grievance procedure and seniority, and nothing more. Having recently won trade union rights after years of struggle, Shanker was unwilling to give up these rights so easily.

The conflict, however, must also be seen in light of the historic failure of the labor movement to address issues of racism and discrimination. For much of its existence in this country, the labor movement had not only allowed racism to exist in its ranks, but was often openly supportive of it. For example, the famous union label, which was long the tool to ensure that companies utilized union labor, was born in the 1880s to keep out Asian workers. Industrial unions such as the steelworkers often negotiated internal work rules and seniority provisions that kept African-American workers locked in the worst jobs in the mill. In New York City, construction unions defended preferential white access to jobs throughout the 1960s. The Brownsville conflict cannot be understood without taking the long and unfortunate history of racism within the union movement into consideration. The fact that groups within the black community saw teacher unions in the light of the racist history of American trade unionism should not be a surprise. Certainly, the response of Albert Shanker did not help matters.

Ultimately, the union won the strike, but lost the war, setting back the cause of teacher unionism. Many of the UFT leaders saw themselves as liberal, and were wounded by the response of the black community. Ties with the African-American community, which would be essential in the coming years, were irretrievably damaged as the UFT became a symbol of narrow racist unionism.

Enforced Narrowness

Prior to the establishment of collective bargaining laws, while many strikes were over the bread and butter issues of wages and working conditions, public workers often struck over issues that were important to them philosophically. For example, teacher unions often sought to impact issues such as class size, disciplinary policies, or educational programs. New York City social workers, during their 1965 strike, included clothing grants among their demands. Caring intensely about their work, public workers often gravitated towards issues that motivated their membership, and dovetailed with the public good.

At the same time, employers and politicians understood that they could gain an advantage by forcing unions to bargain over narrow items such as wages instead of larger ideological matters, where unions could garner public support. Employers therefore pushed legislation making the broad social issues underlying many public employee strikes impermissible subjects of bargaining. These were not mere legal arguments over technicalities related to the scope of bargaining, but intensely political fights over the control of workers, and, indeed, the role of human labor in society. One law review article put forward the management viewpoint on narrowing public employee bargaining:

> A scope of bargaining test that is too broad allows public employees to demand bargaining over issues which usurp public rights. These bargaining discussions, in the form of collective bargaining agreements, are essentially taken directly to the legislature with little opportunity for the public to express its concerns.... Therefore, collective bargaining agreements which concern public issues divest the public of their right to determine those issues.[25]

Public employers believed that workers should not have input into the running of public entities, and that managers insulated from the day-to-day realities of the job should make all the decisions. This represented a hierarchical view of how human society should function, one sharply at odds with the instincts of public workers, who wanted some control over their work. For many public workers, particularly teachers, the notion of public service had motivated their choice of careers. Unlike administrators, teachers have direct, day to day ties to their pupils.

In attempting to justify the restrictions placed on public workers, employers relied on the argument that bargaining on these issues constituted an improper delegation of authority.

However, this is a false argument, as legislators delegate authority in all types of matters. To take a current example, promoters of school privatization support the delegation of the running of publically-funded schools to private charter school operators. It is not consistent to say that the delegation to charter schools is permissible, but allowing far more limited bargaining by public teachers is not.

This issue of the scope of bargaining played a large role in the Chicago teachers' strike of 2012. For years, the city's public schools had been starved for funds by a series of Democratic Party insiders with strong ties to the corporate world. Arne Duncan, who was CEO of the Chicago public school system before becoming President Obama's Secretary of Education, was an enthusiastic supporter of school privatization via charter schools. Rahm Emanuel, formerly President Obama's chief of staff, upon election as mayor adopted a combative stance against the Chicago Teachers Union, vigorously promoting charter school privatization.

With a newly elected reform leadership, the Chicago Teachers Union systematically reached out to the community. Leading up to the strike, the union raised issues such as the lack of school nurses, large classroom sizes, and the future of public education in the city. Once they struck, Emanuel attempted to paint the teachers as greedy, concerned only about issues of pay. These charges of narrowness were especially galling since, at Emanuel's urging, the Illinois state legislature had amended the state's Educational Labor Relations Act to specifically limit the subjects teachers could bargain over. The legislation, which only applied to teacher bargaining in Chicago, said the union could not negotiate over issues such as class size, layoffs, methods of testing students, and length of the school year.[26] Even as Chicago teachers were voting on their strike demands, Emmanuel headed to court seeking an injunction, arguing the strike was illegal because the union was striking over issues of public policy.

Although the strike was settled before the court delivered a ruling, the dispute points to the problems with the narrow scope of bargaining legally allowed many public workers. Lois Weiner argues in *The Future of Our Schools: Teacher Unions and Social Justice* that the limited bargaining imposed on public sector unions has harmed the ability of teachers to impact school policy. Weiner notes that prior to the passage of limited scope of bargaining laws, in schools with a strong union presence, teachers could influence matters of educational policy. With a formalized bargaining structure in place, teachers have less influence over these issues.[27] While Lerner's proposition that unions had more input before collective bargaining is debatable—teacher unionists in the early 1960s certainly would not agree—it is clear that the restricted scope of bargaining has caused teacher unions to become narrow-minded in their contract demands, (though we saw some movement on this front during the teacher strike wave of 2018.) Reviving public employee unionism includes challenging this imposed narrowness. If labor allows management to define its concerns, the outcome will be an uninspired and powerless labor movement. It is only when organizers push beyond the current legal constraints that public unionism can achieve its true potential. This is not just a matter of making political alliances, but of also challenging the management-inspired structure of bargaining.

"Fuzzy" Social Unionism

Despite a rich history to draw upon, a "fuzzy" version of social unionism has emerged today as the main alternative to the work-place-based, struggle-oriented unionism the labor movement once had, and so desperately needs again. Proponents of this modern form of social unionism have to varying degrees replaced workplace activism with community ties, arguing that unions must work with community groups to engage in campaigns for issues like living wage statutes or increasing the minimum wage. Efforts such as the AFL-CIO-sponsored "Working America" go door-to-door in working class neighborhoods signing up members, without a direct connection to the workplace. Others have abandoned the labor movement altogether in favor of organizing around broad class-based concerns.

While all of these are laudable efforts, each represents the abandonment of traditional trade unionism. This point was made by labor historian Nelson Lichtenstein, who took aim at this new push towards community unionism. "Going back to 1855, the idea of a union was people at work get together in some fashion and say we want 'X'" Lichtenstein writes, adding that, "If unions [became] just voluntary associations that are politically active, why are they unions?"[28]

The question that must be asked is where has the "unionism" in social unionism gone? Historically, unions have been groups of workers organized in a variety of ways to impact the wage structures of individual employers and/or entire industries, and to provide more control for workers over the time they spend expending their labor. Unions have differed from other organizations of the working class such as labor parties in that they focused on directly confronting employer power. If labor abandons its historic mission of collective bargaining and workplace organizing, who will carry out these tasks?

The other alternative—one few labor contemporary leaders are willing to address—is to confront the system of labor control. This would require leaders to tackle the difficult task of building a workers' movement capable of violating labor law, reviving an effective strike, and creating the conditions for a mass upsurge. Despite recent upsurges such as the "red state" teacher rebellion, for much of the last two decades, the labor movement has done exactly the opposite. Trade unionists have rarely talked about the restrictions on the right to strike and have adopted pragmatic strategies designed to function comfortably within repressive labor laws. That is why studying the history of public employee social unionism can help show the contemporary labor movement what real social unionism looks like. The examples in this chapter were rooted in the workplace and in the strike. Workers themselves forged connections to the community. Despite the constraints of labor law—or rather perhaps because of them—public workers devised innovative tactics capable of directly confronting employers in the workplace. In the end, the social unionism of the 1960s and 1970s was not a replacement for the strike, but a critical part of strike activity.

5. THE INSIDE STRATEGY: BLUE FLU, WORK TO RULE AND OTHER NON-STRIKE TACTICS

With striking illegal, public employee groups of the 1960s and 1970s were forced to engage in sickouts, slowdowns and other tactics that attempted to steer clear of directly confronting strike prohibitions. A full-blown strike directly challenged governmental authority in ways politicians and public employers could not ignore. In contrast, non-strike tactics allowed politicians and employers to look the other way and pretend workers were not actually striking.

Some public workers found it preferable to avoid the use of the word "strike" altogether. For many professional employee groups such as teachers, the use of euphemisms made striking more palatable. "Teachers often refrain from using the term 'strike' to describe their work stoppage," one commentator noted, "preferring instead to stress the protest aspect of their action by means of such substitutes as 'professional protest' or 'sick leave protest.'"[1] At its 1962 conference, the National Education Association endorsed the use of "sanctions" in which the organization urged teachers not to work in a particular school district, resign as a group, or "withdraw professional services."[2]

While today's labor activists can learn much from these historical precedents, we must remember that these tactics were products of a particular place and time. During the late 1960s, a rising public workers' movement could often get away with work actions that today's trade unionists would be hard pressed to replicate. A generation ago, public employers would often turn a blind eye to a sickout; today, employers launch witch-hunts against public employees they consider to have engaged in such an action. In the context of an ascendant public employee labor movement, workers were able to push the boundaries of the law. Without a legal framework governing bargaining, and with a strong private sector labor movement backing them up, public employees could get away with using more militant tactics. Yet times change, and unions must deploy tactical flexibility in employing actions that worked well in the past under more hospitable conditions. As PATCO strikers learned the hard way, conducting an illegal work action during the beginning of the anti-union Reagan administration in 1981 had very different repercussions than a strike at the highpoint of the 1960s protest-era would have. As a result, any group contemplating such tactics today needs to seriously consider the bargaining and political climate.

Despite the risks, with public employee unionism under attack like never before, rediscovering the full range of tactics used by a previous generation of public workers is more important than ever. Additionally, with trade union strategy becoming more divorced from the workplace, studying the tactics in this chapter will remind public employees of the importance of the historical struggle for the shop floor.

The "Blue Flu," "Red Rash," "Chalkboard Fever" and Other Public Employee Ailments

In 2011, with Governor Scott Walker proposing to slash public employee bargaining rights, teachers in Madison, Wisconsin called in sick for several days to attend protests at the state capital. It was estimated that two-thirds of Madison's teachers reported to the capital rather than to work.[3] Although there were threats of repercussions, there were no reported terminations related to this thinly disguised strike. The teacher sickout became a key component in building the Wisconsin worker uprising that captivated the nation nearly a decade ago. Similarly, in 2019, teachers in Nashville and Louisville also engaged in sickouts, in lieu of a strike, which is illegal in both cities.

In adopting the sickout as their strategy, teachers in Wisconsin, Nashville and Louisville chose a venerable public employee tactic. During the 1960s and 1970s, public employees often preferred the sickout over an all-out strike. By deeming their job actions as sickouts, public employees avoided the types of confrontations with the law that would have been entailed by an official strike. The sickout also allowed the parties to the dispute to save face. Public officials could act as if the job action was not a strike, while unions could maintain plausible deniability. In comparison, by conducting an openly illegal strike, the union was thumbing its nose at the law. This could often make reaching a settlement more difficult because the government employer would be in essence condoning the illegal strike by negotiating with the union.

Police and firefighters, who lacked the legal "right to strike and rarely attempted outright walkouts because of the risk of a public backlash," have long engaged in sickouts. In 1966, New York City police officers engaged in a coordinated sickout in "in which five groups took turns reporting sick on a different day of the week."[4] The New York police followed this up with a wildcat sickout in 1971. The term "blue flu" is generally credited to the Detroit police sickout of 1967, which went on for a week and involved 565 out of 2,668 officers calling in sick. After at first suspending 200 officers, the police department relented, reversing the suspensions and "negotiat[ing] a 10 day truce, out of which came pay increases that set a pattern across the country."[5] The Police Association of New Orleans used the sickout to great effect in 1969 when "[o]ver six hundred (600) commissioned police officers participated in a 'Blue Flu.'" In response, members of the Internal Affairs Division of the New Orleans Police Department and the department's official surgeon "forced their way into policemen's homes in the 'wee hours of the morning' and while police wives protested, the 'sick' cops were ordered by their superiors to submit to medical examinations right then in their own bedrooms." Despite this hostile treatment, the police union did not back down and eventually won amnesty for the strikers.[6]

Other public workers soon developed similar "ailments," such as firefighters who caught the "red rash." With New York City firefighters embroiled in a bitter contract dispute in November 1971, "over 200 new sick claims were filed daily."[7] Teachers came down with "chalkboard fever," which inexplicably prevented them from coming to work. Even air traffic controllers became sick en masse, conducting a series of sickouts from the mid-1960s through their fateful 1981 strike.[8]

While workers could get away with sickouts during the height of the public employee union movement, by the late 1970s, officials had started taking a harsh view of the tactic, with many judges finding sickouts to be thinly veiled illegal strikes.[9] In recent years, police in Toledo, Detroit, Fresno and numerous other cities have been accused by their departments of engaging in sickouts. In 2009, the police chief in Cincinnati was furious when one-quarter of the city's patrol officers called in sick the day after police union members packed a city council hearing to protest police layoffs.[10] The police union claimed the officers had gotten sick because they were stressed out by the impending layoffs. In April 2010, the city of Toledo failed to convince the Ohio State Employment Relations Board that officers were engaging in a sickout in response to contract concessions being pushed through by city officials under the guise of a fiscal emergency.[11] As these examples show, the sickout can still be a successful strategy—though workers must be cognizant of the fact that management is more aware of, and hostile to, the tactic than they were years ago.

The Inside Game: Slowdowns and "Work to Rule"

Many of the non-strike strategies employed by public workers of the 1960s and 1970s fell under what was termed "the inside game." In this version of "striking," workers stayed on the job but either failed to perform some or all of their job functions—known as a "slowdown"—or else performed them too well, adhering exactly to the rules, dubbed "work to rule." The purpose of inside game strategies was to pressure employers "by withholding all or a portion of labor service, similar to that of a strike," the ultimate goal being "circumvention of the law by use of tactics not strictly barred by legal mandate."[12]

An example of a slowdown occured in the early 1960s, when the Police Benevolent Association (PBA) was locked in a protracted battle for union rights in New York City. When Police Commissioner Stephen Kennedy began firing police officers for moonlighting, the PBA stripped him of honorary membership in their association "and offered to pay the fines of penalized members." The commissioner responded by ripping up his PBA membership card "and threatening to dismiss anyone who accepted PBA funds to pay their fines." The union escalated the conflict by engaging in a ticket-writing slowdown.[13] In 1966, New York City police turned to "work to rule" during contentious contract negotiations, "scrupulously report[ing] all street defects, including potholes and broken curbs, and refus[ing] to issue traffic violations or drive vehicles with the slightest safety defects."[14] In 1971, New York City firefighters adopted this tactic "by obeying all traffic laws, including stop signs and stoplights."[15] Four years later, Baltimore police began enforcing a law that required "reporting found objects of value." As a result, police officers began turning in "lengthy reports on pennies found along the sidewalk, or transported obvious pieces of tobacco to the police lab for drug analysis and ticketed many times the number of cars as normal for rarely enforced parking violations."[16]

Other law enforcement employees engaged in their own creative inside game tactics. The police union in Knoxville, Tennessee "threatened to conduct a 'pray-in' by attending Evangelist Billy Graham's Crusade every night, unless the city council took positive action on its proposal for a 40-hour week with 48 hours' pay."[17] Police in Oklahoma City, in the lead-up to a short 1975 strike, conducted a traffic ticket slowdown and a radio silence action, where officers refused to respond to or even acknowledge radio calls.

The inside game strategy wasn't limited to law enforcement. In 1967, members of SSEU in New York engaged in what was known as a "work-in" where employees "were asked to report for work and keep busy doing anything but their regular duties. 'Do not answer the phone, do not pick up a pen or pencil, to not do intake."[18] Despite its originality, the tactic proved to be unsuccessful; after the city suspended 1,100 members, the union settled for mediation of its disputes, and needed the help of other unions to get the suspended workers reinstated. Teachers and graduate students have used similar tactics as well, with the refusal to submit grades being a favored strategy. In 1989, teachers in Los Angeles refused to turn in grades and attendance records. When that failed to produce a settlement, the teachers struck.[19] In other instances, teachers have refused to perform coaching duties or supervise afterschool events.

Perhaps the most creative use of the inside game strategy was by the San Diego County Employee Association, which declared "Human Error Day" in 1979 to pressure the county for a contract settlement. The clerical workers announced that they planned "to work only as hard as they get paid to—by mistappling, misfiling, and generally bungling anything that comes across their desks." The union circulated a flyer urging members to do "what your low pay and no recognition indicate. For what we're paid, you get people who make mistakes, so let's give them what they want—MISTAKES."[20] One suggestion was to issue a permit for a new landfill on the county supervisor's lawn—by mistake of course. According to the local union president, some employees were so enthusiastic about the action they began making mistakes on the Friday before the strategy was set to begin.

Despite the creativity involved, inside game tactics have inherent weaknesses. Depending on the occupational groups involved and the intransigence of the employer, partially withdrawing services or slowing down may not have enough of an impact on operations. Additionally, trade unionists have to contend with potential employer discipline. In the private sector, the courts have long held that such tactics are not protected by labor law, meaning employers are free to discipline or discharge workers for engaging in what are considered partial strikes. Likewise, public workers can be disciplined or fired for engaging in inside game tactics.

Mass Resignations

Another strategy that public workers of the 1960s and 1970s engaged in to avoid "striking" was submitting their resignations simultaneously "to effectuate compliance with their demands."[21] The idea behind "mass resignations" was that, even though the law might prohibit them from striking, nothing could prevent workers from exercising their right to quit their employment. Obviously, the workers did not wish to resign or have their resignations accepted, but merely wanted to avoid the use of the term strike. While the strategy had the inherent danger that employers could accept the resignations, it was nonetheless an important tactic during the early period of public employee strikes.

During a 1968 teachers strike in Florida, in an effort to skirt the state law against public employee strikes, 34,000 of the 55,000 members of the Florida Education Association (FEA) "submitted token resignations, thereby closing 22 of the state's 67 school districts….Overall, half of Florida's pupils were excused from classes, and for many pupils who continued to attend, school was not business as usual."[22] However, after the FEA ended the job action, many individual districts accepted the resignations and refused to allow the teachers to return to work. Leaders of the strike later acknowledged that submitting mass resignations was a mistake, as it exposed their members to retaliation. As one study of the strike noted, "in retrospect, the resignation tactic not only failed to circumvent the legal issue, but it placed striking teachers in the rather vulnerable position of having voluntarily unemployed themselves."[23]

A more successful use of the mass resignation tactic occurred in 1966 in Washington State, when teachers refused to submit their annual reemployment contracts, in effect resigning en masse. Every year, teachers were required to sign personal contracts with the school district for the following school year. In Yakima, with the union trying to force the school board to agree to a first contract, the Washington Education Association drafted a power of attorney for individual teachers to agree to have the union represent them in negotiations for their contracts. The union received 495 such authorizations, representing 95 percent of the teachers, and was able to use the threat of mass resignation to pressure the school board to reach an agreement without calling an all-out strike. Teachers in the communities of Bellevue and Vancouver, Washington soon copied the tactic. None of this was without potential harm, however. As one account cautioned, "It was a risky process because a determined board could attempt to selectively fire teachers who did not turn in a signed contract by a specified deadline."[24]

Unfortunately, the tactic of "mass resignations" did not fool courts or employers. In a number of instances, courts declared such mass resignations to be illegal strikes.[25] For example, when New York City teachers struck in 1967, the teachers claimed it was a not a strike because they had placed their resignation forms in the hands of the union. The court rejected the distinction, and considered the action a strike.[26] Additionally, as we have seen, the tactic left striking workers vulnerable to employer retaliation. When workers went out on a full-blown strike—even if illegal— public officials were forced to take affirmative action to fire striking workers and suffer the political repercussions. In the case of mass resignations, however, strikers themselves quit their positions, and if the strike failed, placed themselves in the position of trying to get their jobs back. As a result of this inherent risk, the tactic of mass resignations was soon abandoned by public employee unionists.

Political Strikes

In many countries, workers frequently strike over political issues, such as a change in the retirement age or the privatization of public services. Such political strikes differ from economic strikes in that workers are not striking over immediate economic benefits, but over issues of public policy. For example, in 2012, many unions in Europe engaged in political strikes against austerity measures, arguing that the working class was not responsible for the financial crisis.

Even though political strikes are generally considered acceptable forms of worker protest in the rest of the world, in the United States such strikes are not considered legitimate by the legal system, as American labor law is specifically constructed to depoliticize and narrow labor strife. As such, laws typically limit the ability of public workers to strike over political issues such as school funding or educational policy.

Prior the enactment of modern public employee bargaining laws, many early teacher strikes blurred the line between political and economic strikes, taking the "form of protest 'to' the public or the legislature rather than 'against' the school authorities."[27] With state legislatures typically providing much of the funding for school systems, separating political issues from immediate economic needs was often impossible.

The most dramatic political strike was the aforementioned 1968 Florida statewide teachers strike. Attempting to force the governor and legislature to increase education funding, 35,000 teachers walked off their jobs, shutting down twenty-two school districts, including the ten most populous in the state. The teachers struck not over immediate contract demands, but rather over the political issue of school funding. Teachers lobbied the legislature, seeking funds for pay increases and to address the underfunding of the state's schools. Republican Governor Claude Kirk and the Democratic legislature did appropriate some money for raises, but this fell short of what the teachers were seeking. The teachers "responded to the legislative disappointments with increased militancy," forcing Governor Kirk to convene a special session of the legislature to address school underfunding. Although the legislature approved $310 million in new taxes, and approved record increases in educational funding, members of the union "were furious because they viewed the pay raise as inadequate and felt teachers were being blamed for a tax increase even though some of the revenues were not for education." On February 16, 1968, the Florida Education Association "called the nation's first statewide strike of teachers."[28]

The striking teachers immediately faced the combined hostilities of the state government, local officials and the media. Several local school boards obtained injunctions to end the strike, and "prepared plans to fire striking teachers." Strikers were also "subjected to numerous forms of petty harassment: loan payments were collected with excessive promptness, strikers' families were threatened, and halls reserved for teachers' meetings suddenly were not available."[29]

In the face of this pressure, the strike was called off after three weeks, with mixed results. The strikers did not win an increase in educational taxes, and in smaller districts, teachers were fired when the school districts accepted their mass resignations. The teachers did, however, prevent a veto of the educational funding bill by Governor Kirk, and also won a resolution allowing school boards to recognize teacher unions. The strike was also credited with bringing collective bargaining to public employees in Florida. As one account noted, "the momentous events of the teachers' strike in 1968 inaugurated a period of major change in public employment in Florida. Increasingly, public employers voluntarily chose to bargain with unions, and public employees no longer hesitated to strike for union recognition or higher wages."[30]

Unfortunately, the politicized vision demonstrated by Florida teachers in 1968 never took hold with teacher unions, and bargaining remained largely confined to individual school districts. Not that there weren't attempts to expand the scope of bargaining. In the early 1970s, David Selden, president of the American Federation of Teachers, promoted what he called multi-level bargaining. Selden argued that to raise pay and standards, teachers needed to band together and attack the main authority, which was the state legislature, rather than underfunded school districts. However, Selden's broad vision of unionism did not square with the increasingly conservative views of Albert Shanker, Selden's former comrade-in-arms during the New York teacher strikes of the 1960s. Shanker ousted Selden as AFT president and turned the union sharply towards the right, becoming a strong supporter of the AFL-CIO's foreign policy agenda which placed the interests of United States' corporations over creating real ties with genuine worker movements in other countries.

Over the years, teachers did occasionally strike over issues of education funding, including a 1964 teacher strike in Utah. Hawaii teachers also engaged in a one-day strike in 1972 regarding the state Department of Education's "alleged failure to hire additional teachers to reduce class size, guarantee duty-free lunches, and provide preparation periods."[31] Nearly twenty years later, teachers in Washington State again adopted the strategy, conducting what they called a "multi-local strike." In January 1991, more than seventy local associations authorized a union plan to engage in simultaneous local strikes to demand legislative approval for new educational funding.[32] For two months, the union built up to the strike, making advanced strike preparations and conducting a publicity campaign. Finally, on April 19, 1991, "more than 13,000 WEA members flooded the Capital grounds in Olympia."[33] The newspapers called it "one of the nation's largest" teacher strikes, as for nearly two weeks, "more than 30,000 members were actually on strike. More than 370,000 students were affected by the action."[34] The immediate results of the strike were not apparent, as it was called off after the governor sent the legislature home with no action on the union's agenda. The following summer, however, many of the proposed cuts to education were reversed and "about $9200 was added to the budget per striking member. Time would prove that the WEA had emerged more successful than was immediately apparent to most when the strike ended."[35]

More recently, thousands of teachers in Wisconsin struck to defend their right to collective bargain. After Governor Scott Walker announced plans to curtail collective bargaining rights in 2011, leaders of the Madison teachers union engaged in an intensely political strike aimed at defending collective bargaining from attack by a rabidly anti-union governor and legislature. As

Jane Slaughter and Mark Brenner note, "The decision by Madison teachers to walk off the job, soon joined by the statewide teachers' union, was the linchpin in the Wisconsin struggle. The strike raised the bar at the outset. It set an example of anger, militancy, and sacrifice (Madison teachers lost four days' pay) and swelled the ranks at the capital."[36]

One-Day, Rolling, and Minority Strikes

In the private sector, one-day strikes offer more protection for employees, since employers cannot permanently replace striking workers. Yet, since the goal of a private sector strike is to impact production or otherwise economically harm an employer, such strikes have minimal impact. Given the political nature of public employee strikes, however, one-day strikes can often be a successful tool.

Some of the earliest New York City teacher strikes were one-day affairs, timed for political effect. For example, the 1960 strike which established the United Federation of Teachers as the representative of New York City teachers was a one-day strike. Likewise, many of the Chicago teacher strikes of the 1960s lasted only a day or two. Because of the novelty of the tactic, the strength of the local labor movement, and the popularity of the public workers' causes, public employees of that era could often prevail with short strikes. In contrast, in areas where the private sector labor movement was weak, such as in the South, many public employee strikes became protracted battles. Although there were twice as many strikes in the Midwest as in the South from 1965 through 1969, the southern strikes were longer, resulting in more lost days, because "government employers in the South put up greater resistance to union demands than employers in the Midwest."[37]

In addition, since a public employee union does not need to stop production, it was not unusual to see a minority of the workforce involved in a public employee strike. Thus, the New York teachers' strike of 1960 was done with a fraction of the union's membership, only jumping to about fifty percent participation in the 1962 strike. Many of the early PATCO strikes were also minority strikes. In the private sector, a strike in which only half the workers participated would be seen as a dismal failure, but because of the different, more political nature of public employee strikes, workers could make impressive gains even with low numbers.

Another innovative strike tactic used by public sector workers was the rolling strike. A good example of a rolling strike was conducted by the Oregon Public Employees Union (OPEU), an affiliate of the Service Employees International Union, in the 1980s. Though this union of Oregon state workers had never struck—despite threatening several times—entering bargaining in 1987, union activists were pushing for a change. At the center of their contract demands was the issue of pay equity. The largely female membership of the union built ties with women's groups through the Pay Equity Action Coalition, and organized a rally of 800 workers and supporters at the state capital in early 1987. Heading into the summer, workers began to organize "demonstrations and actions in the workplace that escalated the involvement of workers in the bargaining process." The workers "picketed in front of their office buildings, sent delegations unannounced to supervisors' offices, and demonstrated around specific worksite issues. As it became clearer that a strike was unavoidable, the activities became more militant."[38]

Rather than conduct the all-out strike that management

was prepared for, organizers instead conducted a rolling strike where, without advance notice, groups of state workers went out in waves.[39] Workers on the coast went out first, followed by the inland valley. Convincing workers to agree to such a change in tactics took much internal discussion. As the union leadership made clear in its newsletter:

> ...the strike plan will involve every member of the bargaining unit. But that involvement will come at different times and for limited periods of time. To strike strategically and smarter, we must identify the areas of management's greatest vulnerability. Then, like skilled surgeons, we must dissect the target. Secondly, we must never underestimate the opponent. The state is strong, but we can undercut its strength by acting unpredictably. We must 'outthink' management by disrupting where they least expect disruption.[40]

After eight days of rolling strikes, the state settled, with workers receiving $9.6 million more than management had offered before the job action, including pay equity increases and the preservation of seniority rights.[41]

From sickouts to slowdowns to mass resignations and rolling strikes, public employee unionists engaged in a variety of non-strike tactics in the 1960s and 1970s. Although not everything they tried was successful, one common feature of these activities was that they required extensive membership participation. By learning to work together toward a shared goal, public employee unionists learned about concepts such as solidarity and self-organization. Ultimately, what was more important than the success or failure of a particular strategy was confronting a set of repressive labor laws which often denied public workers the fundamental right to strike.

6. PUBLIC EMPLOYEE BARGAINING AND THE RIGHT TO STRIKE

Until the late 1950s, public employees were afforded fewer rights to collectively bargain and strike than private sector workers. Judges and politicians of the time argued that the nature of public employment was different from that of the private sector and, consequently, it was illegitimate for public workers to engage in collectively bargaining and striking. As labor scholar Joseph Slater explains, "In the public sector through at least the late 1950s, judges across the nation were unwilling to permit government employees to bargain or to strike, and courts routinely upheld bars on their organizing."[1]

Historically, there were several arguments made against public sector collective bargaining. One was that public officials were giving away their "sovereignty" by bargaining with public employee unions. The right to govern, this argument went, belonged exclusively to elected officials. By agreeing to union contracts, elected officials were said to be impermissibly giving up some of their inherent power—or sovereignty—because "permitting government workers to strike surrenders, to a special interest, government authority to determine public policy."[2] In his 1994 book *The New Unionism in the New Society: Public Sector*

Unions in the Redistributive State, anti-union author Leo Troy offered a far-reaching interpretation of the sovereignty doctrine, stating that, "sovereignty was breached when government extended exclusive representation and the right to consult or negotiate with the government employer over terms and conditions of employment."[3] According to this "non-delegation" argument, by negotiating with a union, public employers were delegating decisions that public officials should be making on their own. Joseph Slater echoes this point, writing how "courts held that public employers could not delegate any power to a private body such as a union. Delegating to labor the power to bargain or to arbitrators the power to bind governments would violate constitutional doctrines and, ostensibly, threaten democracy."[4]

The sovereignty argument proved popular with the legal system. For example, in 1949, a court in Ohio melodramatically declared that "the government is a servant of all of the people. And a strike against the public, a strike of public employees, has been denominated . . . as a rebellion against government. The right to strike, if accorded to public employees . . . is one means of destroying government. And if they destroy government, we have anarchy, we have chaos."[5]

However, public officials enter into thousands of contracts every day, delegating a wide range of governmental functions, from the building of highways to the running of prisons to the provision of healthcare, even the job of fighting wars. If a rule of non-delegation was applied to all contracts, government would grind to a halt. Seen in this light, it is hard to understand how it is an improper delegation to bargain terms and conditions of employment with public workers.

This argument makes even less sense when one considers the privatization of services that is so prevalent. Take, for example, road construction. If a city needs to pave its streets, it can have its own employees perform the work, in which case the workers would be directly under government supervision, even if they were unionized. Alternatively, the government could enter into a contract with a private contractor to perform the work and delegate the entire responsibility to the contractor. Which instance involves a greater delegation of powers? Clearly, the answer is dealing with a private contractor, because both the management and actual performance of the job is being delegated to a third party. By comparison, public employees, whether they are unionized or not, would still be supervised by city personal and the project would be under city control. Yet, the argument is made that government employees, who work for the government under the direct supervision of government officials, are engaging in an illegitimate assumption of authority by negotiating the terms of their employment contracts. Simply put, as one court stated in 1985, this does "not correspond to modern reality."[6]

In recent years, there have been several examples of government delegating public work to private concerns, often to the detriment of the general public. In 2006, Mitch Daniels, then the Governor of Indiana, signed a seventy-five year contract giving a private firm control over the state's highways.[7] The private corporation was also given the authority to increase tolls. As a result, by 2011, tolls on the state's roads had doubled, whereas in the two decades prior to privatization, they had not been raised once.[8] Forner Chicago Mayor Richard Daley, in a similar move, leased the city's 36,000 parking meters to a private company for a term of seventy-five years. Parking rates soon soared and the deal became wildly unpopular, especially when the private firm began demanding tens of millions of dollars from the city in hidden fees.[9] There are many other examples of this kind, such as the privatization of the public school system via charter schools, which involves delegating the duty to educate our children, or the privatization of the prison system, which allows private entities to use force to detain people.

Public Employees Elect Their Employers

Another argument that is made against public sector collective bargaining is that public employee unions elect their bosses.[10] As stated in a anti-union book popular in conservative circles, Mallory Factor's *Shadowbosses: Government Unions Control America and Rob Taxpayers Blind*, "Government employee unions use politics to elect their own bosses—the government officials, like mayors and governors, who will be the actual bosses of the union members. And union members get to fire bosses who don't perform for them."[11] Along the same lines, anti-public employee union advocate Daniel DiSalvo argues that unions end up "handpicking those who will sit across the bargaining table from them."[12]

This "elect their own bosses" argument does not hold up because government officials regularly enter into contracts with airlines, highway construction companies, defense contractors, and other such concerns. These contracts are negotiated with citizens who, just like public employees, vote to elect politicians. Many of these contracts are highly politicized. Major military contracts, for example, are hotly contested and among the bidders are corporations heavily involved in the electoral process. Arguably, with their greater resources, these corporations have a larger ability to deliver votes and influence politicians than do unions.

To take an example from a famous public employee battle, a major backer of Wisconsin Governor Scott Walker's campaign against collective bargaining in 2011 was billionaire David Koch. Major funders such as Koch regularly give millions of dollars to elect the very officials they frequently engage in contracts with.[13] A widely criticized provision of the law restricting union bargaining rights in Wisconsin turned the state-owned power plants over to private corporations—a sector Koch is heavily involved in—without even engaging in a bidding process.[14] Despite this, there was no doctrine that said that a corporation or individual who gave money to Wisconsin's elected officials could not conduct business with the state. It is a double standard to single out labor unions in this regard.

Ultimately, the underlying objective is to curtail the political activities of public employees by hurting them financially. Many who argue against public employee unions are obsessed with the political expenditures of public employee unions. In *Shadowbosses*, Mallory Factor spends several chapters outlining labor unions' alleged domination of political campaigns, ignoring the fact that billionaires and corporations far outspend labor unions in such campaigns. Factor, like many who oppose public sector unions, is fixated on the question of union dues, suggesting his focus is not really on the policy of public sector bargaining, but on crippling those he considers to be political opponents.

For example, in reference to education, Factor suggests one "line of attack is to hit unions where it really hurts—the dues income that they extract from teachers."[15] Indeed, attacking the dues income of public employee unions has been a key component of the anti-collective bargaining movement in recent years. Scott Walker's legislation prohibited the deduction of union dues, allowed "free riders" not to pay for the cost of union representation, and required unions to recertify. A 2013 analysis by the *Milwaukee Journal Sentinel* revealed that union membership declined more than 50 percent at many Wisconsin public employee unions following the passage of Walker's anti-collective bargaining legislation.[16]

Fostering Resentment of Public Employee Unions

Perhaps the most popular argument against public employee unionism is not a legal one, but is based on economics. According to this market-driven theory, "in the private sector, high labor costs tend to be held down by completion and consumer product demand…in the public sector, no such market constraints exist, because public services are monopolies."[17] As a result, public employee unionism should not be allowed because public workers would have far too much power in the market—indeed, are monopolies—and there would be no way to check their influence over public employers.

This argument focuses on the competitive pressures that private sector unions face as compared to private sector unions. As Daniel DiSalvo argues, "In the private sector, the wage demands of union workers cannot exceed a certain threshold: If they do, they can render their employers uncompetitive, threatening workers' long-term job security."[18] According to this theory, even if unionized autoworkers are successful in negotiating salary increases, they would eventually face competitive pressures from a non-union wing of the industry. Public sector workers, on the other hand, do not face such competition and therefore are not subject to "market pressures that might keep unions' demands in check."[19]

There are several problems with this perspective. The first is that it is simply not true that public employee unions do not face competitive pressures. This argument was effectively addressed by the California Supreme Court in *County Sanitation Dist. No. 2 v. Los Angeles County Employees' Assn.*, a 1985 decision holding that public employee strikes were not illegal in California.[20] The case stemmed from a 1975 strike of sanitation workers in Los Angeles in which the county had sought an injunction and damages against the union. The trial court granted the injunction, and awarded the county over a quarter million dollars in damages. Though the strike was settled after eleven days, the county refused to drop the damage claims. The case wound its way through the courts over the next decade, finally reaching the California Supreme Court. In a detailed decision, the Court rejected the idea that there was an unstated rule against public employee strikes rooted in policy doctrines such as the sovereignty argument, noting it to be "a vague and outdated theory."[21] The Court ruled that a "prohibition against public employee strikes is inconsistent with modern social reality and should be hereafter laid to rest."[22] The ruling noted many factors "serve to temper the potential bargaining power of striking public employees" starting with the fact that "wages lost due to strikes are as important to public employees as they are to private employees." The Court also stated that the "the public's concern over increasing tax rates," and the threat of subcontracting both put pressure on unions.

The second major objection to this argument is that it assumes that a particular form of market-driven economics should be the norm for labor relations. According to labor economist Bruce Kaufman, traditional trade unionists and labor economists long understood that "if unions can organize all competing firms, they can use collective bargaining to establish uniform labor costs across the industry ... and thus take wages out of competition."[23] For that reason, eliminating destructive competition was a key objective of trade unionists. Yet, anti-public union activists assume that today's largely de-unionized private sector should be the model. However, public employee unions have long argued that government should be the trendsetters, pioneering concepts such as comparable worth or establishing a living wage for public workers. Representative Keith Ellison of Minnesota and forty-nine other members of the House of Representatives sent a letter to President Obama in September 2013 demanding that he issue an executive order establishing a living wage for workers at federally-funded subcontractors. The letter noted that "the federal government now funds over two million jobs paying under twelve dollars per hour—more than Walmart and McDonald's combined."[24] This struggle highlights the problem in letting the "market" determine pay rates for government jobs.

Public Employee Labor Rights

The basic question underlying all of these arguments is whether public employee bargaining and striking is a right enjoyed by unions, or a privilege granted by politicians and judges. During the heat of the battle over public employee bargaining rights in 2011, Governor Scott Walker claimed "that collective bargaining is not a right; it's an expensive entitlement."[25] If one agrees with Walker, then bargaining rights are privileges that can be taken away.

Public employee unionists of the 1960s and 1970s saw the right to bargain and strike as fundamental human rights which politicians did not have the power to restrict. In May 1967, public employees in New York City filled Madison Square Garden for a rally against the state's proposed Taylor Law, which would penalize public workers for engaging in the right to strike. Three major New York City unions passed a resolution, stating "[t] hat no one, no body of legislators or government officials can take from us our rights as free men and women to leave our jobs when sufficiently aggrieved: when a group of our members are so aggrieved, then indeed they will strike."[26] True to their word, New York City teacher and transit unions violated the Taylor Law multiple times during the 1970s and early 1980s.

The "right to strike" has long been a bedrock principle of the labor movement. It has spurred workers to action and given them the resolve to defy the authority of employers. It has been wielded as a weapon by groups ranging from industrial workers in the 1930s to teachers and other public employees in the 1960s and 1970s. Trade unionists believed fervently in it and were willing to put their liberty on the line to preserve it. Unfortunately, the right to strike is no longer regarded as an essential aspect of trade unionism by the labor movement. Despite this, there is remarkably little discussion of the issue in labor circles. As John Samuelson, President of New York City's Transport Workers Union Local 100 asked in 2012: "Will we fight for public workers' right to strike? Many public union leaders would prefer not to deal with the issue."[27] Samuelson notes that many public employee leaders prefer to focus on electing Democrats or relying on arbitration to settle contract disputes. But with politicians of both parties imposing austerity and attacking public employee bargaining, public employee union leaders can no longer afford to ignore the significance of the right to strike.

Before we discuss the right to strike, we must first understand where "rights" come from. Often, in political discussions, one will hear people asserting various rights, such as the right to bear arms, property rights, the right to choose, etc. Like many matters in the public sphere, there is substantial disagreement among legal and political theorists as to the proper source of these rights. Some believe that rights in this country come from the Constitution, while others look towards international law. Still others believe that rights emerge from basic standards of universal morality. Unsurprisingly, the rights someone believes are often based more on their political perspective and/or concrete interests than on lofty precepts of philosophy. Like many political or philosophical topics, this debate hinges on the outcome one wishes to achieve through exercise of the rights they believe in. In other words, one's material interests tend to shape one's belief—or disbelief—in a particular right or rights. As British labor historian Eric Hobsbawm points out:

> Groups of people who expect to enjoy certain entitlements rarely bother to demand what they already have. The rich do not have to bother about the right to free or cheap medical treatment.It is the poor who have to. Labour movements are concerned with people who have cause to demand a lot of rights, and that is why, irrespective of the philosophical attitude to 'natural law', political theory, or the legal theory of justice and rights, they have played a very large role in the development of human rights.[28]

Thus, a billionaire industrialist opposing federal regulation may believe in "states' rights" while an employee in one of his factories may believe in the right to strike. Which rights ultimately "exist" is not just a philosophical argument, but represents political choices and, importantly, the beliefs of groups in society. Hobsbawm writes that "a 'right' is something which must be recognized as such by other people."[29] In short, a right exists because large segments of society believe in it, and make others believe in it as well. We then gain a right by organizing enough people to believe in it, too. By asserting particular rights, we make choices about the world we want to live in and how we want our society to be structured.

Trade unionists understood that the right to strike was essential if workers were to have any ability to influence wages. The reason is simple—the labor market is too big for the vast majority of individual workers to have leverage on their own. The idea that collective bargaining—and the associated right to strike—was necessary to give workers a say in corporate-dominated society was a key aspect of labor policy in the United States in the 1930s. One of the justifications for the 1935 National Labor Relations Act was that the inequality of bargaining power between individual workers and "employers who are organized in the corporate or other forms of ownership association…tends to aggravate recurrent business depressions, by depressing wage rates and the purchasing power of wage earners in industry."[30] The Supreme Court at the time shared this view, stating in the 1939 case *NLRB v. Jones & Laughlin Steel Corp.* that:

> Long ago we stated the reason for labor organizations. We said that they were organized out of the necessities of the situation; that a single employee was helpless in dealing with an employer; that he was dependent ordinarily

on his daily wage for the maintenance of himself and
family; that if the employer refused to pay him the wages
that he thought fair, he was nevertheless unable to leave
the employer and resist arbitrary and unfair treatment;
that the union was essential to give workers opportunity
to deal on equality with the employer. [31]

Only through collective bargaining backed by the right to
strike could ordinary workers influence wage standards. The right
to strike, in this conception, was a collective right—the right of
workers to band together to take on giant corporations.

Unfortunately, in recent years, many supporters of labor
have attempted to convert collective labor rights into individual
civil liberties. Richard Kahlenberg and Moshe Marvit argue in
Why Labor Organizing Should Be a Civil Right that labor rights
should be made into a civil right enforceable in the federal
courts, like civil right statutes.[32] While there is much to com-
mend in Kahlenberg and Marvit's approach—such as focusing
on the role of legal restrictions, and rejection of the National
Labor Relations Board as a protector of labor rights—ultimately
their viewpoint is damaging to the labor movement. As union
lawyer Jay Youngdahl states, "It is not hyperbole to say that the
replacement of solidarity and unity as the anchor for labor justice
with 'individual human rights' will mean the end of the union
movement as we know it."[33] The problem Youngdahl identifies is
that labor rights are not individual rights; they are group rights.
To be effective, labor rights need to be exercised collectively and
must trump other individual "rights" such as the right to cross
picket lines or otherwise undercut solidarity. By seeing the right
to strike as a group or class right focuses on the distribution of

wealth and power in society.

Historically, the right to strike was viewed as a subset of a larger struggle between labor and capital. By definition, the right to strike is an action against capital. Capital refers to those who own and control the vast majority of wealth in society. Throughout labor history, they have been called capitalists, owners, corporate America, or most recently, the "one percent." Whatever they're called, capital has traditionally been hostile to the right to strike, as it derives its power and wealth from driving down wages and profiting off the labor of working people.

This understanding of the class-based nature of labor rights reaches back to the earliest trade union federations. For example, the preamble to the 1886 Constitution of the American Federation of Labor states that:

> Whereas, a struggle is going on in all the nations of the civilized world between the oppressors and the oppressed of all countries, a struggle between the capitalist and the laborer, which grows in intensity from year to year, and will work disastrous results to the toiling millions if they are not combined for mutual protection and benefit.[34]

One hundred years later, in 1985, California Supreme Court Chief Justice Rose Bird in *County Sanitation Dist. No. 2 v. Los Angeles County Employees' Assn*, noted the class-conscious values that the right to strike was based upon, writing that

> The right to strike was initially regarded as labor's counterpart to the massive economic power concentrated in the corporation. With the rise of monolithic business en-

terprises, it could no longer be maintained that employees' freedom to compete in the labor market as individuals would be sufficient to protect their liberty interests.[35]

Indeed, in a society where workers do not have the right to strike, wealth becomes increasingly concentrated in the hands of a few. With the market determining wages, businesses are then able to relentlessly drive down wages and working conditions in a never ending race to the bottom. This is exactly what we are experiencing in the United States today. According to the Economic Policy Institute, "inequality, which fell during the New Deal but has risen dramatically since the late 1970s, corresponds to the rise and fall of unionization in the United States."[36] With the increasing concentration of wealth comes economic instability as the economy lurches from crisis to crisis. In turn, corporations take their amassed wealth and turn it against society, flooding the political system with money, perverting the economy and dominating the media.

Because of the growing imbalance in equality, trade unionists must once again champion the right to strike as a key tenet of labor philosophy, and convince large sections of the working class that it is important. Do we want to live in a society dominated politically and economically by large corporations? Do we believe that workers are expendable inputs into the production process, or that they have a right to the product of their labor? In this light, the right to strike becomes part and parcel of the fight for the future, and very much a central part of trade unionism.

The Right to Strike Is Grounded in the Constitution

To try and get the concept of the right to strike on the radar of today's labor movement, public employee unionists can look to the United States Constitution. In that vein, the best argument for a constitutional right to strike comes from the aforementioned decision of Chief Justice Rose Bird in the *County Sanitation* case. In her ruling, Bird wrote that

> The constitutional right to strike rests on a number of bedrock principles: (1) the basic personal liberty to pursue happiness and economic security through productive labor ... (2) the absolute prohibition against involuntary servitude and (3) the fundamental freedoms of association and expression.

According to Bird, these specific provisions of the Constitution require that workers have the right to strike. Unfortunately, her arguments have not made much headway through the legal system over the last thirty-plus years.

Overall, there are pros and cons to looking to the Constitution as a source of labor rights. In the positive column, the idea of constitutional rights is fairly engrained in popular consciousness, even if there is lack of agreement on specifics. So, to the extent a labor right is viewed as a constitutional right, there is widespread acceptance for those rights. On the negative side, the Constitution was written by a minority of the population—property-owning, white males, including slaveholders. As such, it has an inherent bias towards capital and against working people. For that reason, finding Supreme Court cases upholding a constitutional right to strike is difficult. As legal scholar James Pope notes, "Given the importance of the question, one might expect that the United States Supreme Court would have issued an authoritative opinion or opinions concerning the status of the right to strike under the U.S. Constitution."[37] Yet, as Pope points out, only a mostly forgotten case from 1923 comes close to upholding the right of workers to strike, and that was an imperfect decision at best.[38] In contrast, decades of anti-labor decisions by lower court judges have rejected a constitutional right of workers to strike, and as Pope writes, "U.S. law is extraordinarily unprotective of the right to strike."[39]

However, just because the courts have not upheld a constitutional right to strike does not mean that trade unionists should not claim that one in fact exists. Certainly, public employee unionists of the 1960s and 1970s asserted as much, even while knowing that few judges were willing to uphold those rights. For example, in a 1970 pamphlet, the American Federation of Teachers addressed the question of a constitutional right to strike by stating that, "Many legal authorities in the area of civil liberties believe that such laws and rules violate the 1st, 4th, 13th, and 14th Amendments to the United States Constitution, but it is highly doubtful that the Supreme Court would uphold an appeal by teachers at this time."[40]

Since the courts have for the most part not adopted these constitutional arguments, why then should labor activists continue to make them? James Pope argues that

> [a] generation of lawyers has grown up and entered practice since the Constitution last played a major role in labor law. Lawyers have become accustomed to thinking of labor law as a practical field in which the grand principles of constitutional jurisprudence have no place. Like much of the received wisdom in labor law, however, this view is ripe for reconsideration.[41]

The reason to believe in a fundamental, constitutional right to strike is not because labor is likely to achieve victories in court any time soon. That simply is not going to happen given the increasingly conservative nature of the judiciary. Rather, the point is to convince labor activists—and the legal system—that the right to strike is a fundamental principle of the labor movement. Public employees in the 1960s and 1970s believed that restrictions on their right to strike were illegitimate, and they were therefore justified in defying judicial injunctions. Only by embracing a similar, militant theory of labor rights can today's labor movement—public and private—justify the confrontational and illegal tactics necessary for its revival.

7. PRIVATIZATION AND THE "FREE MARKET"

During the fiscal crisis of the late 1970s, public employers began to look more and more toward contracting out public services. Initially, these "privatization" efforts were concentrated upon peripheral functions such as food and janitorial services. By privatizing such services, public managers argued that their financially strapped agencies could save money and concentrate on their core functions. Over time, however, privatization expanded well beyond these fringe services. A 1995 survey of America's largest cities found that 50 percent privatized solid waste collection, 48 percent contracted out building security, and 40 percent outsourced street repair.[1] As of 2007, 25 percent of municipal public services in the US were provided by corporations and nonprofits.[2]

No area is safe from privatization, as formally public mental health clinics, grade schools, even the running of prisons, have alin many cases been transferred to private hands. As a hospital worker and local union president in the 1990s, I confronted a privatization effort at the University of Minnesota Medical Center. The hospital was a premier research institute as well as a provider of public health services to poor communities. Despite a vigorous fight by our local union, the university administration teamed up with a non-profit hospital chain to privatize the medical center.[3] (Several years later, when I was a negotiator for the Illinois Nurses Association, nurses and janitors successfully teamed up to beat back an effort to privatize the clinics at the University of Illinois Hospital and Health Sciences System.)

The increasing efforts to privatize public services present a number of concerns for the labor movement. The most obvious is that privatization means a loss of unionized public employee jobs to non-union private companies. Beyond that, privatization also puts pressure on public employee unions during the bargaining process, as public employers can use the threat of privatization to gain concessions. At a more fundamental level, privatization seeks to destroy the public sphere. As public education or the management of prisons is transferred to private companies, something is lost for society as a whole.

One can see the damaging effects of privatization over the past few decades by examining the shift in federal employment to non-union private contractors. In 1993, Democratic President Bill Clinton launched an initiative known as the "National Partnership for Reinventing Government. " According to a 1999 report on the initiative, Clinton was able to shrink the federal civilian workforce to its smallest size "since Kennedy held office and, as a percentage of the national workforce, the smallest since 1931."[4] Overall, the size of the federal workforce "shrunk by nearly 20 percent relative to total employment during the Clinton years."[5]

In addition, federal employment shifted from being largely unionized to an increasingly subcontracted workforce in the 1990s and 2000s. From 1999 to 2005, while the size of the federal workforce remained relatively stable, the use of contractors expanded rapidly, rising from an estimated 4.4 million in 1999 to 7.6 million in 2005.[6] Today, federal contractors outnumber federal employees by a ratio of four to one. Although the rate of unionization of public workers remained steady, the public sector itself shrank, leading to what Richard Hurd of Cornell University calls a "creeping deunionization under the guise of privatization."[7] The numbers back this up: In 1953, there was one federal employee for every 78 workers in the economy overall; by 2009, there was one for every 147.[8] With similar privatization efforts underway in cities and states across the nation during the 1990s, the percentage of public workers relative to the economy shrunk significantly. Hurd writes that while "the public sector accounted for 17.51 percent of total employment," in 1991, by 2001, "this share had dropped by almost one-tenth to 15.85 percent."[9]

Worst of all, despite it being one of its stated rationales, privatization does not in fact save employers money. A 2011 study of the privatization of federal jobs revealed that a contracted worker costs 1.83 times more than a federal worker.[10] Not only do private contractors cost more than their federal counterparts, but, due to lax oversight, private contracts are often subject to massive amounts of fraud. A 2013 study by the non-partisan Congressional Research Office determined that an estimated "$31 billion and $60 billion was lost to contract waste and fraud in contingency operations in Iraq and Afghanistan."[11] All of this does not begin to address the social costs of privatization, which include the elimination of good-paying jobs and the diminishment of fair employment standards which benefited millions of public workers over the years.

Public Enemies

One of the most insidious aspects of privatization is that it creates entire industries which seek to profit from the public interest. Think of any policy debate around privatization and hidden in the weeds are powerful firms looking to make money. As a 2012 report from People for the American Way summarized:

> In recent years, dozens of privatization initiatives have been proposed, passed, or implemented. They are aimed at water treatment, transportation infrastructure, education, prisons and prison services, health care and other human services, government buildings, municipal maintenance, emergency services, and more. Those efforts are frequently promoted by the same Wall Street firms that helped create the recession and financial crisis; by right-wing foundations, think tanks and political donors who are eager to exploit the budget balancing desperation of public officials; and, of course, corporations eager to tap public coffers and take over assets built with taxpayer funds.[12]

A web of right-wing foundations, private contractors, and powerful corporations are seeking to capture public resources and institutions which generations of Americans have built. For example, public education has long been a core service of government. Public schools were created from the efforts of reformers who fought for the right for all children to receive an education. Yet, in the past few decades, different factions

> ...have teamed up to wage a long-term assault on public education. For some, privatizing education is primarily a religious or ideological project. For others, the billions

of dollars that flow through public schools is a tempting source of cash, from outsourcing meals and transit to vouchers and other tax schemes to send tax dollars to private schools. For some it's both.[13]

Powerful interests funded by some of the richest individuals in this country promote the privatization of the public school system. According to prominent education analyst Diane Ratavich, "[m]ajor foundations, including the Walton Family Foundation, the Bill and Melinda Gates Foundation, the Eli and Edythe Broad Foundation, the Michael & Susan Dell Foundation, and dozens of others lavished funding on the expansion of charter schools and charter chains."[14] In the case of education, privatization directly attacks one of the most highly unionized major job categories in the United States, teachers.[15] Charters schools, by contrast, are overwhelmingly and often viciously non-union; currently, just over ten percent of charter schools are unionized, and most charter school operators vigorously oppose unionization.[16]

This rabid anti-union philosophy is based on the charter school movement's belief that teacher unions are at fault for the problems in the nation's education system.[17] At a deeper level, charter schools are part of a vast program to eliminate the public sector. Milton Friedman, the right-wing economist, speaking of an effort to divert funds from public schools to private sector institutions, stated that, "Vouchers are not an end in themselves; they are a means to make a transition from a government to a free-market system."[18] Charter schools proponents are motivated not by concern about America's children, but by hostility to the public sector, in particular since the evidence overwhelmingly shows that charter schools do not provide a better education than public schools.[19]

Another industry where privatization has taken hold is the prison system. Prisons used to be considered one of the core functions of government. But, beginning in the 1990s, a private prison industry began to develop in this country. As Michael Brickner and Shakyra Diaz of the ACLU of Ohio write, "In 1990, only a few years after private prisons first began to proliferate, 7,000 prisoners were housed in private facilities nationwide. In June 2010, the number rose to 126,000 prisoners, or 9 percent of the nation's total state and federal prison population."[20] Private prisons pay their guards less than government-operated institutions, and also have greater turnover and less experienced staff.[21] The focus of private prisons is on increasing profits, not on safety or rehabilitating prisoners. Bricker and Diaz note that "[p]rograms such as drug counseling, mental health care, and job training diminish their [private prisons] profits. Private prisons have no incentive to rehabilitate individuals either, as their livelihood depends on more people being incarcerated, not less."[22]

Privatizing the criminal justice system also introduces corrupting influences into what should be matters of basic human freedom. In a particularly egregious case, Mark Ciavarella, a judge in Pennsylvania, was sentenced in 2013 to twenty-eight years in prison for receiving millions of dollars of bribes in exchange for sentencing over 5,000 juveniles to lengthy sentences in private institutions.[23] These types of scandals extend to the influencing of government legislation, which was evident when it was revealed that the Corrections Corporation of America (now called CoreCivic), a major private prison company, was pushing legislation to extend prison sentences and incarceration in order to fill their jails and increase their profits. CoreCivic attempted to disguise its efforts by working through the American Legislative

Exchange Council (ALEC), "a nonprofit organization that functions as a matchmaking service between corporations and public officials who are eager to take care of each other's interests. ALEC, funded by corporations, CEO-funded foundations and extremist ideologues like the Koch brothers, invites corporate lobbyists to write model legislation with and for rightwing state legislators."[24] ALEC was forced to cut ties with the CoreCivic when it was revealed the company was promoting "bills that privatize prisons, expand the use of low wage prison labor, extend the sentences of prisoners (and occupancy rates) and increase detention of immigrants."[25]

Citing such dramatic cases is meant to highlight what happens when the profit motive is introduced into decisions of whether to forcibly detain persons and deprive them of their liberty. Former educator and blogger Anthony Cody explains some of the problems with turning public prisons over to private entities, noting that "prisoners are the ultimate disenfranchised citizens, with very little power over their conditions. Corporations that run prisons literally have a captive audience. There is growing evidence that prisons run for profit are even more dangerous for inmates than those run by state agencies."[26]

A Defense of the Public

Joining the profiteers in pushing privatization is a highly ideological group of conservative activists who do not believe that the public sphere should even exist. Once relegated to the extreme right of the Republican Party, these activists have seen their views increasingly adopted by the mainstream of the GOP—as well as some centrist elements of the Democratic Party—in recent years. According to Richard Hurd, these ideologues support "the dismantling of large segments of the government bureaucracy so that privatization becomes the end rather than simply a method to improve effectiveness."[27]

In order to push forward their agenda, these enemies of the public sphere have carefully crafted a message over the past thirty years that the "free market" is the natural state of affairs. In this view of the world, government is necessary to a very limited degree, and mostly represents an intrusion into the rightful order of things. Yet, there is there is no such thing as a "free market." Author Alex Marshall debunks the notion of "free market" economics in his book *The Surprising Design of Market Economies*, in which he states that "the term 'the free market' is really a slogan masquerading as a neutral description."[28] According to Marshall, the concept of the "free market" has slipped into the political discussion without being challenged, despite the fact that "there are no 'free' markets, in any meaning of the word, whether free as in open, or free as in costless."[29] To quote Thom Hartmann, the progressive radio and TV host on the same topic:

> In actual fact, there is no such thing as a 'free market.' Markets are a creation of the government.Governments provide a stable currency to make governments possible. They provide a legal infrastructure and court systems to enforce the contracts that make markets possible.They provide educated workforces through public education, and those workers show up at their places of business after traveling on public roads, rails, or airways provided by government....And, most important, the rules of the game of business are defined by government.[30]

The idea that the market should govern every aspect of human activity is a relatively new phenomenon. In his book *What Money Can't Buy: The Moral Limits of Markets*, Harvard philosopher Michael Sandel points out that "there are some things money can't buy, but these days, not many. Today almost everything is up for sale."[31] He adds that, "the logic of buying and selling no longer applies to material goods alone but increasingly governs the whole of life."[32] To Sandel, over the last three decades we have seen "an expansion of markets, and market values, into spheres of life where they don't belong. To contend with the situation, we need to do more than inveigh against greed; we need to rethink the role that markets should play in our society."[33]

Rethinking that role needs to be the job of public employee unions. At the end of the day, the campaign against the public sector is highly political and ideological. It represents the ascendency of capital's ideas within the political space, and the concurrent marginalizing of left-wing or socialist-minded ideas that helped spur the labor movement into being. In the broad sweep of history, just as conservatives have sought to reshape public policy by injecting their "free market" ideology into all realms of civil and economic society, labor must fight back by articulating the importance of the public sphere while delegitimizing the notion that the private sector is better or somehow more natural. Over the course of several decades, bedrock union ideas such as "labor creates all wealth," "human labor is not a commodity," and notions of labor freedom have been abandoned by many trade unionists. Reviving the labor movement therefore will require a fundamental rethinking and restating of how the public—i.e. unions—is greater for the good of society than the private—i.e. "the free market."

8. STRIKING AND THE LAW

With public employee unions increasingly operating in an environment where their basic rights are being outlawed, an awareness and appreciation of how previous generations of public workers coped with repressive labor laws is vital.

Many in the union movement today look back to the formative labor battles of the 1930s for inspiration. However, those historical struggles—when gritty industrial workers in teeming urban centers revolted against large industrial concerns—happened so long ago as to barely seem relevant. Indeed, the battles of the 1930s were closer in time to the Civil War (seventy years) than they were to the present day (nearly ninety years).

For many public workers, the uprisings discussed in this book are much more instructive, and can help answer one of the key questions for public employee unions: namely, what effect do restrictive labor laws have on strike activity? This is not a mere academic point, but addresses important issues of strategy. Should unions focus on electoral politics and building a broad progressive movement to influence policy? Or should they foster direct action, grassroots organizing and militant challenges to labor law? Looking to the actions of their predecessors in the 1960s and 1970s can offer today's public workers important insight into these questions.

Rejecting Restrictions on the Right to Strike

As will discuss in detail later in this chapter, whether public employee strikes are outlawed or not has little effect on strike levels. Public worker strikes were illegal in the 1950s, yet, with no
changes in the law, strike activity exploded during the 1960s. If
legal restrictions were what mattered most in determining strike
actions, one would expect to find changes in the law prior to a
rise in strikes. That does not mean that legal restrictions are irrelevant; rather, as the experiences of public workers in the 1960s
and 1970s demonstrate, it is worker attitudes towards the law
that make all the difference. In other words, it is the willingness
of the union movement to violate labor law that is important,
rather than the law itself. And, a half century ago, a militant generation of public employee unionists rejected the idea that they
needed to comply with legal prohibitions on their right to strike.
This change in union consciousness validated strike activity, and
as we shall see, ultimately forced the law to change to accommo-
date the reality of public employee strikes.

This incredible public employee strike wave consisted of
mostly illegal strikes. Until Vermont loosened restrictions on
strike activity for teachers in the mid-1960s, and Hawaii legalized public employee strikes in 1970, striking was illegal for
public sector workers in every jurisdiction in the United States.
In states such as Ohio, Illinois and California, public employee
strikes were not legally permitted until well into the 1980s. Other
states with high levels of strike activity, such as New York, never
legalized public employee strikes, nor did the federal government.

Despite the prohibitions on striking, public workers nevertheless struck repeatedly during this period. From 1958 to 1968, while not a single state authorized a strike, "the number of public employee strikes increased 17-fold from the previous decade."[1] Adding up the numbers of workers engaging in illegal strike activity easily reaches into the millions, which makes this strike wave one of the largest and most sustained campaigns of civil disobedience in US history, along with the union strike wave of the 1930s, the mass defiance of the civil rights and anti-war movements of the 1960s, and the wildcat strike wave of the early 1970s. Striking workers undertook these actions at great personal risk, as they faced loss of employment, were threatened with fines, and in rare instances, were forced to move or even find different careers. Union leaders risked arrest and imprisonment for violating judicial injunctions. Yet public workers struck anyway.

The key to this massive strike wave was a change in attitude among public workers toward striking and the law. During the 1960s and 1970s, there was widespread demand among public workers that their unions drop constitutional prohibitions on strike activity. This new generation of unionists took their fight to their union conventions, pushing to remove language from union constitutions prohibiting public worker strikes. Through internal battles within their unions, and most importantly, by striking, they forced their national unions to support the right to strike.

Prior to the 1960s, most public employee unions either barred strikes in their constitutions, or had unofficial policies against striking. While the constitution of the American Federation of State County and Municipal Employees (AFSCME) did not specifically prohibit strikes (except for police and firefighters), the policy of the union was to discourage striking.[2] AFSCME's constitution also forbade strikes of public security officers, a rule that the Fraternal Order of Police, the nation's main police union, followed. Similarly, the International Association of Fire Fighters constitution stated that: "We shall not strike or take active part in any sympathetic strike."[3] AFL-CIO officials were also dismissive of the right to strike for public employees, despite union president George Meany's 1955 statement that "[i]t is impossible to bargain collectively with the government."[4]

National teacher organizations also rejected the strike. When the American Federation of Teachers affiliated with the American Federation of Labor in 1916, the new AFT adopted a no-strike policy. This view was reaffirmed in 1934 when the AFT convention upheld the policy against a motion to rescind it.[5] While teachers at the 1947 convention complained that state laws did not allow them to engage in meaningful contract negotiations, the convention nevertheless declared that "despite the existence of these deplorable conditions we deem it advisable that the American Federation of Teachers maintain a no-strike policy."[6] In 1951, the AFT executive board went further, stating that the "funds and facilities of the national union would not be used to support a strike."[7] The National Education Association likewise condemned strikes as violations of teacher's individual contracts.

This attitude changed in the early 1960s with surprising rapidity as a new generation of public employee unionists emerged who were no longer willing to accept their status as second-class citizens. Seeing private sector workers striking repeatedly and making major gains, these militant public workers came to believe that legal restrictions on their right to strike were illegitimate, and that it was acceptable to violate the law. As a result, by the mid-1960s, union prohibitions on strike activity began to fall. AFSCME upheld the right to strike at its 1966 convention for all but police and firefighters.[8] Even the relatively conservative National Education Association and the American Nurses Association reversed course and supported the right of affiliates to strike.[9] In 1968, delegates to the International Union of Firefighters convention removed the strike prohibition by a six to one margin.[10] In doing so, the delegates were simply acknowledging reality—regardless of what it said in their constitution, firefighters were striking anyway. In fact, leading up to the 1968 convention, firefighters won gains in cities such as Atlanta, Youngstown, St. Louis, Kansas City, and Lansing by striking, despite repressive labor legislation.[11] In a two-year period following the 1968 convention, "firefighter local unions engaged in approximately a hundred 'strike situations'" which "included not only actual work stoppages but also strike threats, slowdowns, mass sickness, and other job actions."[12]

Police unions also removed no-strike clauses from their constitutions. Since the failed 1919 Boston police strike, unionization of the police had been considered illegitimate, let alone striking. However, by the late 1960s, sickouts and thinly disguised strikes by police had become commonplace. Reflecting this new reality, AFSCME removed its ban on police strikes at its 1970 convention. Again, this merely recognized the fact that police were increasingly turning to job actions to win their demands. According to one estimate, there were fifty-one police strikes between 1965 and 1969.[13] After police went out on strike with other city employees in Baltimore in 1975, the *Washington Post* reported that, "[t]he clenched fist, the symbol of militants that police often confronted on the picket lines of protesters, now belongs to patrolmen in Baltimore, too, as they march through the streets in their first strike."[14]

Changing to a strike-based strategy created intense conflict within public employee unions, as more militant leaders pushed aside older, more conservative officials who resisted change. Whether on the national level, such as the legendary Jerry Wurf challenging Arnold Zander for the leadership of AFSCME, or the countless local battles within teacher organizations, the intra-union battle over strike strategy was every bit as important as the larger campaigns against employers.

Winning the Right to Strike—By Striking

With outlawing strikes no longer a realistic option, public employers were forced to come up with other methods to try and stem the tide of public employee strike activity. As a result, several states decided to take the opposite tack and legalize public employee strikes. The idea behind this strategy was that by making strikes legal, "they can be regulated and procedures can be required which will reduce the incidence of strikes and shorten those strikes that do occur."[15]

The passage of the first comprehensive state law legally permitting public employee strikes occurred in Hawaii in 1970 (Vermont passed a limited law in 1966), and is an excellent example of how illegal strikes can force slow-moving legislators to act. In 1968, Hawaii's constitution was amended to say that "[p]ersons in public employment shall have the right to organize for the purpose of collective bargaining as prescribed by law."[16] Despite this new constitutional mandate, the state legislature failed to enact legislation in 1969 authorizing collective bargaining. After realizing that such legislation was unlikely, 1,600 state workers took matters into their own hands, striking for two days. The resultant strike "illustrated an increasing militancy among Hawaii's public employees, corresponding to rising unrest on the Mainland, and caused more thought to be given to the collective bargaining process as a way of determining wages and other employment conditions."[17]

In the wake of the strike, the Hawaii state senate commissioned a report in 1970 to study collective bargaining and strike prohibitions. Despite "the near universal prohibition against strikes by public employee in various jurisdictions throughout the country," the report determined that

> ...experience has shown that such prohibitions are ineffective in preventing, and at times have been the cause of, strikes (sic). In many instances, strike penalties have been modified or waived in order to bring striking employees back to work, often times fostering disrespect and disregard of the law. ...The Committee feels that granting the right of public employees to strike will not increase strikes, but on the other hand, would be effective in deterring strikes because genuine collective bargaining would result thereby.[18]

The report underscored that, due to the militancy of public workers, the right to strike needed to be granted. In case state legislators failed to grasp that point, Hawaii's public workers engaged in another statewide strike on the day the legislature was voting on the law. Initially, nurses and other hospital workers stuck for wage increases and in support of the right to strike. The following day, they were joined by members of the white collar Hawaii Government Employees Association. All together "about

13,500 workers…were active in the stoppage; an estimated 7,000 marched on the state capitol. Lack of custodial services and cafeteria workers closed schools. After three days the strike ended with the legislature granting the blue-collar raise and increasing the wages of about half the white-collar workers."[19] And that is how Hawaii's public workers became the first in the nation to win the legal right to strike—by illegally striking.

In Minnesota, teachers gained the right to strike by also engaging in illegal strike activity. Although other public employees in Minnesota were covered by a state bargaining law, teachers were excluded. In 1970, the teachers union in Minneapolis pushed for a change in the law and entered bargaining with a list of demands that included wage increases, prep time for elementary teachers, maximum class size regulations, and the ability to remove disruptive students.[20] When management refused to agree to union demands, the teachers voted to strike. (This would be the third strike for Minneapolis teachers in a little more than twenty years, following a three-week strike in 1948 and a 1951 strike honoring the picket lines of school janitors.)[21] Minnesota state law at the time treated illegal strikers harshly, requiring that striking teachers be fired, eligible only for reemployment with loss of tenure, as well as stipulating that they receive no salary increases for one year following reinstatement.[22] The teachers still struck, settling after three weeks, with program improvements and salary increases. The following year, the Minnesota legislature enacted the Public Employee Labor Relations Act, authorizing collective bargaining for all public workers.

In Ohio, unionists had long lobbied to change state law to permit public employee strikes. The state's Ferguson Act, passed in the flurry of anti-strike legislation in the aftermath of the 1947 strike wave, barred strikes by public employees and forbid government entities from entering into collective bargaining agreements. Despite numerous efforts over the years, attempts to repeal the Ferguson Act had proven unsuccessful.

With no other option, public workers in Ohio began to engage in illegal strikes. From 1974 to 1979, there were an average of forty-seven public employee strikes per year in the state (which included an average of five police strikes annually.)[23] One strike in particular, a dramatic 1979 walkout by Toledo police, firefighters, and municipal workers, is generally credited with convincing reluctant lawmakers to pass a bargaining law.

On July 1, 1979, Toledo's 3,400 municipal employees struck. They were soon joined by the city's police and firefighters, who, fed up with the refusal of the city to bargain, struck for two days. As the *Toledo Blade* later summarized,

> The walkout, on July 1, 1979, led to 48 hours of mayhem in parts of the city, with countless acts of arson, including the firebombing of the former Plaza Hotel on Monroe Street across from the Toledo Museum of Art. Some citizens armed themselves with shotguns and other weapons. A TARTA bus driver was killed and another was robbed, prompting the transit agency's chief to suspend service because he feared for the drivers' safety.[24]

After delaying for a few more years, the Ohio state legislature finally passed a comprehensive law authorizing collective bargaining in 1983, permitting strikes for many groups of public workers, and binding arbitration for those denied the recourse to strike. George Tucker, a union president active in the effort to get the bargaining bill passed, credited the 1979 strike as playing a key role in persuading legislators that the law had to change. "That's what basically led to the collective-bargaining bill ... because the [Toledo] police were on strike. I think this was the one that showed that there had to be some means to get a settlement."[25]

These are just a few of the many examples of the period which demonstrate how public workers won the right to strike by illegally striking. Certainly, in most of these instances, public officials could have responded with repression. They had all the tools at their disposal, such as restrictive labor laws containing harsh penalties, compliant judges hostile to collective bargaining, and a media generally opposed to public workers. Yet, for various reasons, including a relatively strong private sector labor movement, most officials chose to avoid using the repressive powers available to them under prevailing labor laws.

Today, when discussing the necessity of wide-scale violations of labor law, trade unionists will frequently focus only on the worst-case scenario of harsh penalties, including fines and potential jail time. While these are serious considerations which must be carefully weighed, the experience of public workers in the 1960s and 1970s shows how militancy can force policymakers to make difficult calculations on how to respond. If a union has sufficient political support and the overall context is conducive, history shows that public employers may decide to take the route of conciliation, rather than repression.

Legalizing or Prohibiting Strikes Had Little Effect on Strike Levels

In the 1970s and 1980s, labor academics spent a great deal of time and effort trying to figure out how different state laws affected strike activity. Public employee bargaining presented a unique situation for these researchers because they could examine strike activity before and after changes in the law, as well as compare strike levels in fifty states, all with separate collective bargaining laws. The results of this research was succinctly summed up by Richard Kearney in his textbook, *Labor Relations in the Public Sector*: "[S]tates legally permitting strikes have not experienced greater incidence of work stoppages than those that prohibit it."[26] In other words, no-strike laws had little to no effect on public employee strike levels. In fact, public workers actually struck at higher levels where striking was illegal, as "the most comprehensive examination of public sector strike bans and consequent strike activity concluded that job actions are more frequent in states with no-strike laws."[27] In California, for example, there were approximately sixty public worker strikes between January 1969 and July 1972, leading to the conclusion that "the law is not a deterrent to public employee strikes."[28]

In determining strike levels, factors such as the level of organization of the private sector workforce and community support mattered more than legal restrictions. Thus, throughout the 1970s, union strongholds such as New York, Ohio and Illinois saw high levels of public employee strike activity despite the illegality of such strikes. According to a 1985 article in the *Journal of Collective Negotiations*, in the period from 1970 to 1981, "70 percent of the most strike-prone states were those where strikes were not legal."[29] Instead of stopping them, blanket strike prohibitions actually forced workers to strike. Without a framework requiring collective bargaining, the only way public workers could get intransigent public employers to bargain was to strike illegally. The law in turn encouraged public employers to dig in their heels against workers, with the disputes usually centering not on bargaining demands, but on the larger and harder to resolve principle of whether unionization would even be permitted. So, for example, the 1968 Memphis sanitation workers' strike dragged on not because of disputes over wages or working conditions, but because of issues of like dues check off and union recognition.

Ironically, there is some evidence that the passage of laws containing the right to strike actually depressed strike levels. For example, Ohio, as we have seen, and Illinois were relative latecomers in granting the right to strike, passing laws in the early 1980s. One study examined the impact of these laws, determining that legislation permitting public worker strikes did not result in an increase in strike levels:

> Thus, the experiences in Ohio and Illinois run counter to the expectation that enactment of comprehensive public sector bargaining laws containing a right to strike would increase the incidence of strikes.Despite an increase in bargaining activity in the first eight years under the Ohio statute, strikes averaged 13.75 per year, compared with an average of 55.71 strikes per year from 1974 to 1980.In the first eight years of the Illinois statute, strikes averaged 15.75 throughout public education, despite an increase in bargaining, compared to an average of 24.56 strikes per year among K-12 teachers prior to the IELRA.[30]

After looking at a number of other variables that influence strike activity, the study concluded that: "The analysis does not firmly establish that legalizing and regulating strikes decreases their frequency, but does firmly show that legalization does not result in increased strike frequency."[31]

Instead, it was the type of penalties that mattered most in reducing public employee strike levels. For example, New York's draconian Taylor Law did help lower strike activity. (The Taylor Law fines workers two days' pay for each day they strike, with unions losing the ability to check off dues in punishment for illegal strikes.) In addition, it was also found that interest arbitration eliminated strikes and rendered "strike penalties irrelevant."[32] Interest arbitration is a procedure where arbitrators made the final decision on contract terms, often based on a set of legislatively prescribed standards which, not surprisingly, increasingly favor management. In the 1960s and 1970s, most public employee unions opposed arbitration, as it put contract decisions in the hands of a third party.[33]

Overall, the experience of public workers in the 1960s and 1970s shows that legal restrictions have little bearing on strike activity, a point which held true for private sector workers as well. Joseph McCartin examined the rise and fall of private sector strikes in the twentieth century, determining that "history suggests that changes in U.S. strike patterns were not directly correlated with changes in the law."[34] McCartin notes that the militant strike wave of the 1930s commenced prior to the passage of the National Labor Relations Act, and that anti-labor modifications such as the 1938 McKay doctrine allowing permanent replacement scabs and the 1947 Taft-Hartley amendments took decades to have a major impact on strike activity. For that reason, McCartin cautions against placing too much emphasis on the role of labor law in determining strike activity. Instead, what mattered most was the willingness of trade unionists to directly confront legal prohibitions on the right to strike. Whether it was sit-down strikers in the 1930s flaunting state laws protecting employer "property rights" or public workers of the 1960s violating injunctions, understanding and rejecting legal restrictions was what was important. The lesson for today's trade unionists is that just because labor law prohibits strike activity does not mean that workers cannot strike.

9. CHALLENGING UNJUST LABOR LAWS

Every four years, labor unions spend millions of dollars and countless hours campaigning in an attempt to elect a Democratic president. Underlying this effort is the belief that having someone from a "sympathetic" political party in office will help labor reverse its decline. Sadly, this has proven over and over again not to be the case. Union density in the private sector dropped from 20.1 percent in 1980 to 11.4 percent in 1992 under the Republican Reagan and George H. W. Bush administrations.[1] Since then, private sector density has continued to decline at a steady rate, dropping to 6.4 percent in 2018, despite the fact that we have had sixteen years of Democratic administrations during that time. If a change in party affiliation of the presidency mattered for unions, one would expect to see an increase in density under Democratic administrations, or, at the very least, a stable rate of density. The truth is that unions have been getting hammered at the bargaining table for four decades, no matter what party is in control of the White House.

Some of the greatest damage to unions has actually been inflicted by Democratic administrations. For example, the North American Free Trade Agreement, pushed through by Bill Clinton in the mid-1990s, is credited with the loss of over one million jobs, with the job loss concentrated in the manufacturing sector and in highly unionized states.[2] In addition, over 300,000 federal jobs were shed during the Clinton administration as part of the "Reinventing Government" project.[3] Both of these initiatives targeted highly unionized sectors of the economy and contributed to the decline in union density.

On the issue of union bargaining power, there has been little difference between Republican and Democratic administrations, as strike levels dropped sharply with the employer offensive of the early 1980s and continued their decline through the end of the Obama administration. (Things finally changed in 2018 under the viruently anti-union Trump administration, when we saw the largest number of striking workers in thirty-two years.[4]) All of this is not to say that elections are unimportant, or to even argue that labor's electoral strategy is misplaced. Rather, it is to show that the long decline of unionism in this country will not be reversed (or even significantly impacted) by electing more favorable politicians.

Unfortunately, the main impediment to union revival is rarely discussed, even within the labor movement: namely, that the "rules of the game" have been tilting more and more toward management for the past fifty years. In the 1940s and 1950s, steelworkers and miners struck entire industries at once, winning improvements like employer paid health care and pensions. Back then, collective bargaining worked, providing for a higher quality of life for my parents' generation. That is not the case anymore, as decades of anti-labor court decisions and legislative changes have gutted the right of workers to organize and strike. Today, employers can permanently replace striking workers, threaten to move production, and blatantly engage in anti-union activities.

As Chris Rhomberg's excellent account of the 1995 *Detroit News* strike, *The Broken Table: The Detroit Newspaper Strike and the State of American Labor* reveals, the protections of New Deal legislation have been transformed into anti-labor laws that severely curtail effective strike activity.[5] To truly revive the labor movement would require leveling the playing field to prevent employers from interfering in worker self-organization, limiting the ability of employers to move capital to avoid unionization, and restoring the right to strike.

Yet none of these defining "rules of the game" are currently on the policy table. As Rhomberg writes, "political forces in the United States make even modest labor law reform nearly impossible, and the record of union efforts to pass legislation in Congress is not encouraging. Even if laws are passed, they face hostile interpretation in federal courts."[6] With the labor movement currently having no chance to get any kind of favorable legislation passed with a Republican senate and president in power, and with the Supreme Court moving even further to the right, as we saw in the *Janus* ruling, there is little reason to believe that the far-greater changes needed to restore labor's power will become law any time soon.

In many regards, the situation facing the labor movement today parallels the public worker situation of the late 1950s. Back then, public employee unionists attempted to convince workers to join their weak and ineffective unions, lobbied to amend labor law, and appealed to public employers for recognition. Few would have predicted that a few short years later, these very same unions would be engaged in one of the more militant labor upsurges in US history. The need for a similar kind of rebellion should be clear to today's trade unionists. The labor movement is not just in trouble; it is dying. Union density has been falling for decades. As the movement has declined, employers have become emboldened on both the bargaining and legislative fronts to attack remaining union strongholds. And there is no reason to believe that the downward trajectory will be reversed any time soon. While we have seen a recent increase in public worker militancy—particularly among teachers—overall strike activity, especially in the private sector, has not changed.

In light of the many obstacles against it, constructing a labor movement capable of challenging—and even violating—labor law seems like an insurmountable task. After all, how can unions face down the combined might of massive corporations, the courts, the police, and the media? However, during the 1960s and 1970s, teachers, police, firefighters and other public employee groups were able to successfully defy labor law, strike, and win concessions. Their example is one that the contemporary labor movement needs to study, and emulate.

"...tomorrow I'm going to jail, all because of you."

By the mid-1960s, the public worker strike wave was in full swing. In a 1966 editorial, *Time* magazine lamented the rash of illegal public employee strikes, complaining that New York's Condon-Wadlin Act (the precursor to the Taylor Law), which forbade strikes by government workers, was actually ineffective in halting strikes.[7] "Despite all these precedents, New York City last week was paralyzed by a massive strike of public-transit workers." noted *Time*. "As in other recent New York strikes involving teachers, no official dared invoke the Condon-Wadin Act, the nation's toughest anti-strike statute."[8]

In the context of a rising public worker movement, government officials and employers hesitated to respond with repression in the face of worker militancy. If they jailed strike leaders, for example, the tactic could backfire. As Harry Wellington, a law professor at Yale, noted in 1971, "In some situations, the incarceration of a union leader for contempt will turn that leader into a martyr and stiffen support for the strike."[9] Union leaders were actually willing to go to jail for strike activity. As well-known labor mediator Theodore Kheel pointed out, the government's use of repressive tactics "made the march to jail a martyr's procession and a badge of honor for union leaders."[10] Even top leaders of international unions were willing to go to jail for defying judicial injunctions. David Selden, President of the American Federation of Teachers in the early 1970s, ran the international union for sixty days from his jail cell.[11]

Another problem faced by employers and politicians in responding with repression was that it could engender opposition from other constituent groups in society. In their 1977 book *Poor People's Movements*, Francis Fox Piven and Richard Cloward write about how the industrial workers of the 1930s and the civil rights movement of the 1960s "aroused strong sympathy among groups that were crucial supporters of the regime."[12] If the penalties against strikers were too harsh, other groups supportive of labor could become disaffected. Harry Wellington writes about how finding the right mixture of repression was a "vexing problem" for employers and politicians, and that the penalties "must not be so harsh as to engender a feeling of revulsion in the community."[13]

Indeed, during the 1960s, the use of repressive tactics frequently backfired on authorities, triggering expressions of solidarity from the labor movement. For example, one of the longest teacher strikes of the period occurred in Philadelphia and was, as the *New York Times* explained, "an uncommonly nasty one."[14] Two union leaders were jailed, and hundreds of rank and file teachers were arrested for illegal picketing. The major breakthrough in the strike came after police vans fanned out across the city one morning, arresting more than 400 teachers picketing in front of their schools. The teachers were able to win the strike, gaining major pay increases, after the labor movement in the city responded with solidarity. According to the *New York Times*, "[a] key factor that helped open the way to settlement was the support given the teachers by some 40 union locals. Agreement came just 12 hours before the locals were to begin a paralyzing citywide general strike—called 'a day of conscience'—that labor leaders say was needed to counter 'union busting' by the school board."[15]

Similarly, a dramatic display of solidarity from the International Longshoreman's Association helped bring an end to the bitter Charleston hospital workers' strike of 1969. The strike, a classic civil rights public employee struggle, dragged on for months. The Reverend James Lawson, carrying on Dr. Martin Luther King's legacy, ran the support campaign from his prison cell, having refused bail. The strike was settled on the eve of a threatened solidarity walkout by dock workers. While not always this dramatic, the support of the local labor movement would often prove critical in settling public worker strikes during the 1960s and 1970s.

One of the best examples of the collision of worker militancy and government repression occurred in 1973, when teachers in Evergreen, Washington attempted to bargain for their first ever contract. When the school district refused to negotiate, the union's young organizing staff focused on building solidarity among the teachers. "They had to perform at a given level before we moved them to the next. They never underperformed," explained staff organizer John Chase. "They always exceeded everything we asked them to do. When we had a candlelight march we asked for two from each building. Over eighty showed up. We did member surveys, and we had newsletters."[16]

When the union negotiating team determined that worker support was solid, they called for a strike vote to back up their bargaining demands. With strikes illegal in Washington State, the union knew that a vote to strike was also a vote to violate labor law. For the union leadership, in particular, calling for a strike would expose them to jail time. Despite the risks, the vote was overwhelming for a strike, and on May 14, 1973, teachers in Evergreen walked off the job. State Judge Guthrie J. Langsdorf quickly issued an injunction against the strike, hauling union local president Fred Ensman and strike leader Dick Johnson into court and ordering them to send the striking teachers back to work. When they politely refused, Langsdorf sent both of them to jail. The union then appointed teacher John Zavodsky as president. Zavodskly was also brought before Judge Langsdorf, and after declining to order the teachers back to work, was sent to jail, too.[17]

Instead of backing down, the union decided to escalate the struggle. An older teacher, Betty Collwell, was the next person appointed as union president. Prior to appearing before Judge Langsdorf, Collwell addressed the school board and "delivered a powerful speech. She concluded her speech with 'I've never broken the law or had so much as a traffic ticket but tomorrow I'm going to jail, all because of you.' Then she turned and left the room."[18] One school board member broke down crying after hearing Collwell's speech.

To raise the bar even higher, every teacher decided to turn themselves in and dare Judge Langsdorf to arrest them all. Thus, "all of the striking teachers gathered at a park near the courthouse. Each carried a little bag filled with their toothbrush, a book, and underwear."[19] The teachers then marched to the courthouse and demanded to be jailed. With only eleven prison cells available, and worried about bad press, the flustered judge backed down. Langsdorf then turned his anger toward the school board, ordering the board members to appear before him and telling them "that he would put them in jail if they did not bargain in good faith."[20] The school board, no longer able to rely on the court injunction, agreed to a contract settlement, with the union winning many of its demands. (The judge refused to drop contempt charges against the three union presidents; Johnson and Ensman would serve forty-five days in prison, while Zavodsky served forty-three.)[21]

The powerful lesson of the Evergreen strike was that with smart organizing, community mobilization and mass defiance, the law could be successfully violated. This is not to be confused with the purely symbolic, ritualized activities in vogue today, which usually consists of a handful of labor leaders, along with some community allies, sitting down and committing preplanned civil disobedience. Such tactics, although technically illegal, are ineffective when compared with the mass violation of the law that characterized public employee actions of the 1960s and 1970s. As Reverend James Lawson noted during the Memphis sanitation strike in 1968: "Picketing, or poster walking, as such is not any good unless it can help create the confrontation. That means that you can't have in a downtown area a handful of people carry posters. You either have to have hundreds and thousands or you have to move from that to sitting in or some other strategy."[22]

The 1970 Postal Strike—Federal Employees Join the Strike Wave

Another major struggle that can provide inspiration for today's public employee unionists is the 1970 postal strike. Rather than taking place in a rural setting like the Evergreen strike, the postal strike began in New York City and fanned out across the entire country. And while the Evergreen strike involved the state judicial system and the local power establishment, the postal strike drew the attention of President Richard Nixon, Congress, the national media and the federal courts. Despite the differences, in both illegal strikes, workers put pressure on the enemies of collective bargaining, ultimately gaining much of what they demanded.

In an era before faxes, email and the internet, the postal service was critical to the functioning of commerce in this country. However, there was unrest among postal employees in New York City and elsewhere in the late 1960s, as they were grossly underpaid compared to other blue collar jobs. In New York City, sanitation workers earned 27.4 percent more than postal workers, police and firefighters 53.8 percent more, and transit workers 61.9 percent more.[23] As former American Postal Worker Union President Moe Biller stated, "wages were pitiful....working conditions were deplorable—ancient dungeons for postal facilities, with no heat in the winter, no air conditioning in the summer... it was downright medieval."[24]

Years of broken promises to fix labor relations had left postal workers increasingly frustrated. When President Nixon delayed a postal pay increase in February 1970 for six months, the worker's anger began to boil over. In New York City, feelings ran especially high. In 1969, workers in the Bronx had conducted a sickout "to protest an insulting 4.1 percent wage increase granted by President Nixon in an executive order."[25] The Postal Service retaliated by suspending the workers involved, which spurred increased organizing among the union over the following year. Eventually, rank and file activists prepared for a strike within the massive New York local, packing membership meetings. When the local leadership reluctantly held a strike vote on March 17, 1970—without the support of the national union—2,500 members showed up to the meeting and voted to strike.

The strike began slowly on March 18, 1970, "when a handful of letter carriers set up a picket line outside the massive General Post office building in Manhattan...Yet within two days, some 200,000 postal employers joined picket lines in front of post offices throughout the country, making theirs not only the largest strike against the federal government, but also the largest wildcat strike in U.S. history."[26] The strike soon spread from Manhattan, crippling postal service in more than thirty major cities, including Chicago, St. Paul, Detroit, Denver and San Francisco, as well as many smaller communities across the country. As *Time* magazine reported, "the postal strike almost immediately began to strangle the operations of commerce, impair Government functions and vastly inconvenience the public."[27]

Striking was strictly prohibited for federal employees, who were allowed collective bargain over some issues, but not wages. While there had been intermittent strikes of federal workers in the late 1960s, none had approached the size of the postal walkout. With the strike not authorized by the national postal union, local union leaders were up against incredible odds, facing not only their leadership, but also "the federal court system, the president, Congress, the press, and eventually the National Guard" after Nixon mobilized 30,000 National Guard troops and took over the Postal Service.[28] Although the strikers in New York held out for a few days after the National Guard takeover, Nixon's action effectively ended the strike. The Nixon administration did agree to a wide range of improvements, although they were not put in writing. It ultimately took months to get the promised pay increases, which were not quite as generous as they were originally made out to be. However, in the end, the strike won a 14 percent wage increase and collective bargaining rights for postal workers.

The most important outcome of the strike was the mass disobedience and solidarity expressed by the postal workers, which was difficult for the government to handle. As *Time* magazine noted in discussing the strike, "While raising many practical and legal questions, the postal strike also underscores the helplessness of government in the face of organized, even if nonviolent, lawlessness. In spite of state and local laws forbidding such actions, strikes by public employees have spread like an epidemic throughout the nation."[29] In summarizing the effect of the strike, one account wrote about the "extraordinary display of rank-and-file militancy on the part of previously passive workers." Despite the short length of the strike, postal workers "parlayed their militancy into substantial bargaining rights, increased wages, and more powerful and democratic unions."[30]

The examples of the Evergreen teachers and the postal workers reveal an important point about militancy—namely that a strong and aggressive labor movement is worrisome to public employers and government officials. Labor militancy forces the government to take sides between workers and public employers, and to justify it's actions, positions, and laws. Faced with a labor movement defiantly resisting the law, politicians can no longer hide behind the supposed neutrality of the legal system, but must make the difficult choice to intervene on the side of employers in order to resolve the dispute. As Piven and Cloward point out in *Poor People's Movements*, policymakers are compelled to choose between repression and conciliation: "When the government is unable to ignore the insurgents, and is unwilling to risk the uncertain repercussions of the use of force, it will make efforts to conciliate and disarm the protesters."[31] In the 1930s, governors in key industrial states hesitated to use armed force to quash strikes, fearing the response of labor. Writing about those strikes, Piven and Cloward note:

> Yet neither could government run the risks entailed by using massive force to subdue the strikers in the 1930s. It could not, in other words, simply avail itself of the option of repression. For one thing the striking workers, like the civil rights demonstrators in the 1960s, had aroused strong sympathy among groups that were crucial supporters of the regime. For another, unless insurgent groups are virtually of outcast status, permitting leaders of the regime to mobilize popular hatred against them, politically unstable conditions make the use of force risky, since the reactions of other aroused groups cannot be safely predicted.[32]

An insurgent labor movement in the 1930s was able to neutralize the government's ability to utilize force to break strikes. Public workers in the 1960s and 1970s put the authorities to a similar test. Yale law professor Harry Wellington discusses the problems that mass defiance by public workers creates for public employers, noting that although state laws often gave public officials the tools to crack down on public workers, "[h]arsh penalties automatically invoked…run the risk of converting an economic strike into a strike for amnesty that will be difficult to settle without openly abandoning the law."[33] In other words, politicians do not want a strike which is enjoying broad community support to continue; they want it over as quickly as possible.

Refusals to Obey Judicial Injunctions

As we saw in the Evergreen teachers' strike, the judiciary has long played an important role in union-busting. Prior to the labor upsurge of the 1930s, private sector employers would rush into court seeking injunctions to force striking workers back to work. Likewise, public employers in the 1960s and 1970s relied on the authority of judges to bust strikes. The issuance of an injunction was often a critical moment in a strike. If workers obeyed the injunction, they would lose the strike and be vulnerable to employer repercussions.

While the 1968 strike of sanitation workers in Memphis is a major landmark of the civil rights movement and the reason Martin Luther King, Jr. was in Memphis the night he was assassinated, few know that two years earlier, sanitation workers in the city attempted a similar walkout. However, with the workers set to strike, local union leader T.O. Jones called the action off the morning it was to begin after the city secured an injunction and lined up former sanitation workers to cross picket lines. AFSCME International President Jerry Wurf was furious that the workers had called off the strike in the face of an injunction; the labor leader "blew his stack" when he heard about the injunction, saying that, "'It was intolerable that the strike was called without some way of dealing with it, and it was equally intolerable to fold in the middle of the night on that crappy injunction.'"[34]

Wurf's response revealed the strong belief of many trade unionists that judicial injunctions were illegitimate and should be ignored. Today, with most union leaders unwilling to even contemplate violating labor law, the level of support for militant strike activity by the leader of the nation's largest public workers' union seems amazing. Yet, Wurf's position on violating the law was clear: "Never strike in anger or frustration; only strike if you can win. And if you can win, ignore the injunction and go to jail if necessary."[35] To Wurf, what mattered were not the legal restrictions, but the likelihood of success. After being hauled into court for violating an injunction during the 1968 Memphis sanitation workers' strike, Wurf declared, "I have never been impressed with the injunction. If you got the power to win the strike, it's academic. If you ain't got the power, they are going to knock your head off anyway."[36]

Wurf's sentiment was shared by many public employee union leaders of the 1960s and 1970s, who understood that by holding firm, they could often not only win their immediate demands, but avoid harsh repercussions afterward. As Albert Shanker explained while being jailed during 1967 New York teachers' strike, "teachers are not going to give up their fight for professional dignity, and they're not going to give up the fight for good schools, and if this is the price that we have to pay for it periodically then that price is gonna be paid."[37] Shanker believed that injunctions were ineffective, and often had the opposite effect from what the government intended. Speaking of the two jail sentences he received for illegal strike activity, Shanker said that, "The net effect of my punsihment, of course, was to strengthen the union. There's no question that my having gone to jail those two times created a kind of solidarity and togetherness between the membership and the leadership which would not otherwise exist."[38]

Lessons For Today's Labor Movement

Some argue that the time for militancy has come and gone. Labor unions today, they say, lack a tradition of militancy; they are weak, both numerically and ideologically; and they no longer have strong social movement allies. However, the future looked just as bleak for labor in the 1920s and 1950s, when similar arguments were made to discourage strike activity. After a decade and a half of retreat and decline, labor officials of the mid-1930s were a cautious lot who had survived the open shop period of the 1920s, and were thus not inclined to rock the boat. AFL leaders of the time "came to believe that mass-industry workers were unorganizable and that big employers were unbeatable. Defeatism worked against any great release of organizing energy."[39]

Entering the 1960s, the future for public employee unions did not look particularly bright, either. Most public employee leaders preached moderation, urging workers to focus on lobbying legislators and hoping for incremental change. After all, with public employee strikes illegal and laws specifying harsh penalties, how could public workers possibly strike and win? Thankfully for a generation of militant public workers, these timid ideas were ignored.

Today, multiple theories abound as to what it will take to revive the labor movement. Some believe that the focus should be on building a strong progressive movement, while others advocate for the need to pass pro-labor legislation. Some even argue for the development of a "fortress unionism" in which labor simply waits for things to get better, while protecting union strongholds.[40] Rarely, however, is the only historically proven method of union renewal—working class militancy—discussed. Simply put, the labor movement has to fight its way out of its current crisis. When labor does come back, and I strongly believe it will, it will look a lot more like the defiance of the 1960s than the currently fashionable but ineffective strategies popular these days.

Public sector workers can help keep the flames of militancy alive, and by power of example, lead a labor movement based not on cooperation, but on fighting. When public workers fight back, such as in the teacher strike wave of 2018, they can inspire the entire labor movement. Ultimately, the main message of the public worker rebellion of the 1960s and 1970s is one of hope. The first step for today's trade unionists is admitting both the necessity and possibility of breaking free of repressive anti-labor structures. Only then can labor find its way again. Sometimes, struggle breaks free in ways that surprise us, in massive explosions of worker self-activity, which will be the focus of the next chapter.

10. UPSURGE

In his 2003 book, *The Next Upsurge*, progressive activist Dan Clawson argues that labor has traditionally grown through upsurges rather than slow, incremental growth. "Historically, labor has not grown slowly," Clawson writes, "a little bit each year. Most of the time unions are losing ground; once in a while labor takes off."[1] History backs up Clawson's analysis, as the labor movement tripled in size between 1933 and 1941, expanding from 2.9 million union members to 10.5 million.[2] Public employee unions grew tenfold over a twenty-year period, rising from 400,000 members in 1955 to over 4 million in the 1970s.[3] In 1960, fewer than eleven percent of public sector workers were unionized; by 1976, forty percent of the nation's public employees were represented by unions.[4]

These dramatic periods of growth did not happen because of one-on-one organizing, political lobbying, or patiently bringing workers into unions shop by shop. Instead, they were grassroots explosions in which workers redefined their unions, "changing cultural expectations...laws, structures, and accepted forms of behavior."[5] In my thirty years in the labor movement, I have caught brief glimpses of what could be considered "upsurges." Some of the more militant strikes of the last quarter century, such as the

Hormel strike in the mid-1980s, the Pittston strike in the early 1990s, and the "Warzone" in Illinois, had elements of upsurges, albeit on a much smaller scale than those of the 1930s and 1960s. While these contemporary struggles tapped into deep feelings of discontent among the industrial working class and prompted an outpouring of grassroots solidarity, they were limited in scope, being about one contract, and were not connected to a larger movement.

The closest I have been to a true upsurge was the Wisconsin protests of 2011. Living in nearby Minnesota, a friend and I decided to drive to Madison one Saturday during the height of the protests. At first, I was disappointed to arrive just as the official rally was winding down. However, I soon realized that what was going on was something I had not experienced during my time in the labor movement. Individually, and in small groups, workers kept walking towards the capitol building with handmade signs. The typical features of large rallies—the marshals and the set program—were nowhere to be found. Upon entering the building, I saw thousands of people jammed into all levels of the rotunda. If the labor movement rises again, it will probably look a lot like Wisconsin, which contained all the classic components of a labor upsurge—grassroots protest, worker self-activity and a bottom-up character.

Unfortunately, the Wisconsin struggle turned out to be an isolated affair, great while it lasted and over all too soon. Once legislators rammed through the anti-union legislation that had prompted the initial protests, the crowds receded. While some say that union officials diverted the struggle, they fail to understand that upsurges have their own dynamics, which we will examine in detail in this chapter.

Where Do Upsurges Come From?

Social scientists and labor activists have long offered a myriad of explanations for why mass worker protests come into being. Some believe that sudden deprivation causes workers to rebel; for example, the large scale unemployment of the Depression in the 1930s. Others point to rising expectations, or the breakdown of institutions of social control. In *Poor People's Movements*, Francis Fox Piven and Richard Cloward argue that "whatever position one takes on the 'causes' of mass unrest, there is general agreement that extraordinary disturbances in the larger society are required to transform the poor from apathy to hope, from quiescence to indignation."[6]

Traditionally, labor upsurges have developed around major social changes or dislocations in the economy, which unsettle the existing modes of operation and production. Thus, we find that the great strike waves in US history tend to cluster around periods of societal change and upheaval. Several strike waves occurred immediately after the major world wars, when the combination of wage suppression during the war, outrage over corporate war profits, employer aggressiveness, rising inflation, and the militancy of returning battle-hardened troops provided the recipe for labor-management confrontation.[7]

In her book *Forces of Labor*, Beverly Silver analyzes global strike activity from the 1870s through the 1980s, demonstrating that strike patterns generally follow shifts in production.[8] For example, as auto manufacturers shifted production around the world during the twentieth century, strike activity followed along to each of the new regions, from the United States in the 1930s to Europe in the 1960s, Brazil and Korea in the 1980s, and today, as Silver predicted, China. Silver shows that a similar process occurred in other industries such as textiles. Unlike many analysts of globalization, Silver believes that the global economy does not spell the end of class struggle, just its transformation.

Labor Notes co-founder and author Kim Moody echoes Silver's ideas by explaining that general strikes typically have been the result of "disruptions" during periods of worker solidarity:

> The U.S. mass and general strikes all shared similar characteristics. First, they all occurred as part of an existing labor upsurge: 1877, 1886, 1919 and 1946 were all preceded by a growing wave of strikes reaching levels far above those of the previous period. These periods of upsurge were the result of underlying conditions, often major changes in the organization of work and/or disruptions in living standards—not by most accounts, a simple result of the 'business cycle.'[9]

Moody goes on to say that "[e]ach of these strikes began in a different way, but all unfolded in solidarity with strikers under attack. In most of them the question was not whether some official body called the strike, but which group(s) of workers took the next step that set things in motion."[10]

In the last decade, there have been several calls for a general strike. For example, during the Wisconsin protests of 2011, many labor activists argued that the struggle should escalate into a general strike. The Madison-based South Central Federation of Labor even went so far as to pass a resolution calling for a general strike.[11] Despite their hopes, a general strike did not materialize.

Labor educator and activist Cal Winslow believes that the

weakness with calls for general strikes is that they usually do not come out of the working class movement. He argues that an upsurge cannot be created from the outside, but must come from the self-organization of workers:

> Strikes, even the bureaucratic, involve mobilizations from below—implicitly they raise issues of power and control. And the fundamental place of self-activity—and isn't that the point? 'The emancipation of the working class must be the act of the workers themselves.' No one can do it for you; you have to do it yourself. Not the politicians. Not the bureaucrats. Not the church.[12]

Behind every historical labor upsurge was years of patient organizing and agitation. Labor upsurges, like all protest movements, are organized by activists, often toiling away in obscurity and creating the experience and organization to further these battles when they do come. Simply calling for a general strike without having laid a long-term foundation of support will not work.

The Components of a True Labor Upsurge

In *Poor People's Movements*, Francis Fox Piven and Richard Cloward analyze three powerful social movements of the last century: the labor movement of the 1930s, and the civil and welfare rights movements of the 1960s, attempting to "identify the institutional conditions which sometimes make mass movements possible, the institutional conditions which determine the forms taken by mass movements, and the institutional conditions which determine the response of elites."[13] Piven and Cloward conclude that a social movement's ability to succeed does not stem from how many persons are members of supporting organizations, but on its ability to force concessions by disrupting the operations of the system. For the labor movement, that means that what matters is not the level of union membership, but the ability of workers to compel employers to accede to their demands by halting production.

Unfortunately, for the last few decades, the labor movement has argued that what is most important for the health of trade unionism is increasing union density. In the process, the movement has moved away from the militancy that characterized unions during a good portion of the twentieth century. The problem with the quest for mere growth is not just that it has failed, but that it has steered the labor movement further and further from the confrontational tactics that can actually gain concessions from employers—and drive up membership levels.

In examining the labor upsurges of the 1930s and 1960s, there are several common elements present during periods of union growth:

1. A change in worker consciousness towards authority and the law
2. The development of new and more effective methods of struggle
3. The creation of new organizational forms and/or a new wave of militant leadership.[14]

Perhaps the most important of these factors in creating an upsurge is a change in consciousness among working people towards following the law and resisting authority. Upsurges develop when working people develop a belief that defiance is necessary and useful, or as stated in *Poor People's Movements*, "[l]arge numbers of men and women who ordinarily accept the authority of their rules and the legitimacy of institutional arrangements come to believe in some measure that these rulers and arrangements are unjust and wrong."[15] Piven and Cloward add that, in our society, power rests on "an elaborate system of beliefs and ritual behaviors which defines for people what is right and what is wrong and why; what is possible and what is impossible; and the behavioral imperatives that follow from these beliefs."[16]

In the realm of labor, power is based on workers accepting the legitimacy of the system they operate under. Employers and politicians count on people to come to work every day, and for unions to follow restrictive labor laws. During periods of upsurge, however, workers begin to reject existing institutions and demand new ways of doing things. They develop what can be termed a "consciousness of rebellion," which Piven and Cloward identify as including three components:

> First 'the system'—or those aspects of the system that people experience and perceive—loses legitimacy." People began to see signs of authority as unfair and unjust. Second, people who are ordinarily fatalistic, who believe that existing arrangements are inevitable, began to assert 'rights' that imply demands for change. Third, there is a new sense of efficacy; people who ordinarily consider themselves helpless come to believe they have some capacity to alter their lot.[17]

When these ideas become widespread in society, working people begin to defy authority in surprising ways. Unfortunately, today's labor movement has done a horrible job at developing a consciousness of rebellion among workers. In comparison, corporate leaders—with assistance from politicians and the media— have done a masterful job at convincing unions that they can only engage in strikes and other forms of militancy under conditions in which they are guaranteed to fail. While some union leaders grumble about the situation, there is no widespread discussion within the movement about systematically violating labor law. Likewise, while many public sector unionists complain about the restrictions on bargaining and striking, few public worker unions challenge the idea that public employers should not have the power to take away the right to strike. The current system of labor control, in many ways, is legitimized by the compliant actions of today's unions.

Looking back to the public employee rebellion of the 1960s and 1970s, we see clear evidence of Piven and Cloward's three steps toward changing worker consciousness. First, the system of public employee bargaining started to lose legitimacy in the early 1960s as public workers began seeing the denial of their collective bargaining rights and the lack of a right to strike as unacceptable. This rebellious attitude was in stark contrast to the 1950s, when, for example, among teacher unions there was a "widely held view within the profession that strikes were seen as 'conduct unbecoming,' and…that a strike by teachers 'is a triple act of treason' against the profession, the children and the government."[18] As a result of this passive attitude, teachers engaged in only 107 short strikes from 1940 to 1960.[19] Over the enxt decade, these attitudes completely changed, and "by 1970 73 percent of teachers accepted that teachers could and should strike compared with 53 percent in 1965."[20]

Public workers also began to assert their right to engage in collective bargaining, demanding equity with then thriving private sector unions. During the 1960s and early 1970s, collective bargaining in the private sector was relatively stable (at least on the surface), and strikes were accepted as part of the process. Joseph McCartin writes how the "stabilization of private sector labor relations after World War II and the routinization of the private sector strike" made strikes less threatening to policymakers and "opened the door to a reconsideration of unionization and collective bargaining in the public sector."[21] In this context, an expanding public employee workforce began to assert demands for equal treatment, arguing that the right to bargain and strike were essential to end their status as "second class citizens."[22]

Finally, through the power of example, public workers began to see that striking could make a difference in their lives. Solidarity was infectious, and crucial victories led to copycat actions. To quote Albert Shanker: "Perhaps it is a bad lesson for us to learn, but the City has convinced us that striking brings us gains we need and cannot get any other way."[23]

As more and more public employees successfully struck, other public workers adopted the tactic. Labor arbitrator Arnold Zach, writing in 1972, noted that

> ...the demonstrated success of initial illegal strikes such as the New York Transit strike and some early teachers' strikes became powerful proof that the power to strike was of far greater relevance than the right to strike. As long as some employees obtained improvements from the strike, others recognized it as a useful vehicle for their protest as well.[24]

As important as it is for workers, a change of consciousness by itself cannot sustain an upsurge. An upsurge requires concrete victories so that workers can see that fighting back can lead to success. To win a battle, however, typically requires new methods of struggle—a break with the existing system. The qualitative leap forward that characterizes a worker upsurge does not happen by simply doing the same things better. Instead, it requires a sharp break with the status quo. The victories of the 1930s were only possible because unions engaged in new forms of struggle, including the adoption of an industrial form of unionism. The introduction of mass production techniques made the traditional craft union system obsolete, since organizing skilled workers in a dozen or more separate unions—while excluding the vast majority of semi-skilled or unskilled workers—was completely ineffective in the new paradigm. For labor to have any chance of success required the embrace of industrial unionism, which organized all of the workers in an enterprise or industry.

This push for industrial unionism did not just happen by accident, but was the end result of a decades-long campaign by labor progressives. Frequently championed by socialists and other leftists within the labor movement, James Morris writes in *Conflict Within the AFL: A Study of Craft Versus Industrial Unionism, 1901-1938*, that the industrial union resolution "was first introduced in 1901, and the matter never lay dormant for any considerable period of time thereafter."[25] Between 1901 and 1923, "twenty-one industrial union resolutions were introduced into fifteen AFL conventions."[26] The push for industrial unionism wasn't confined to the AFL, as labor progressives pushed rival labor federations that organized skilled and unskilled workers on an industrial basis, including "the American Railway Union, the Socialist Trade and Labor Alliance, the Western Labor Union, the American Labor Union, the Industrial Workers of the World, and the successive trade union arms of the Communist party."[27] Simply put, progressive unionists were unwilling to accept a labor movement incapable of organizing all workers.

However, simply shifting to industrial unionism was not an option, as the movement also needed to devise tactics to ensure that the emerging industrial workers could win their struggles. Withdrawing their labor could not work for trade unionists during the 1930s as it had for craft unions, as employers could easily find scabs to replace unskilled and semi-skilled workers. Here again, labor progressives took the lead in developing the powerful production halting strike, which through mass picketing and sit-down strikes, prevented the employer from operating. These tactics were backed up with militant workplace-based solidarity, which pulled in other workers in the industry or class to fight together. In short, these activists learned how to run strikes, build rank and file organizations, and fight for union reform.

For today's trade unionists hoping for a renewed labor upsurge, these lessons should be instructive. Just as the labor upsurges of the 1930s and 1960s required new forms of union struggle, an upsurge today would require a break with the existing structures. It would require challenging restrictions on solidarity and effective strike activity, as well as a refusal to follow unjust labor laws.

Jerry Wurf and AFSCME's Upsurge

The phenomenal growth of the American Federation of State, County and Municipal Employees (AFSCME), the nation's largest public employee union, offers today's trade unionists an excellent example of what a true labor upsurge looks like. Founded in the 1930s by public employees in Wisconsin, AFSCME expanded dramatically during the 1960s and 1970s through the repeated use of militant tactics like the strike. Going back to the 1950s, however, few would have predicted AFSCME's explosive growth. The union's president at the time, Arnold Zander, a former policy analyst for the state of Wisconsin, favored lobbying and a timid approach toward public officials. Zander did not see the strike as a viable weapon, stating that "the use of the strike weapon would be fatal to accomplishment in public employee organizations. Therefore the strike is not used."[28]

Within AFSCME, however, a militant group of trade unionists was demanding a more confrontational approach. Among these activists was Jerry Wurf, who began his union career organizing cafeteria workers in New York City in the 1940s, helping to form Local 448 of the Hotel and Restaurant Employees International Union (HERE). However, when Local 448, which primarily represented cashiers, was merged into a larger New York HERE local, the aggressive Wurf was fired. As Wurf himself put it: "Being a dumb bastard, I raised questions about the administration of the union, about democratic process....Pretty soon they sent me running."[29] Wurf tried to get a rank and file cashier job to agitate from within, but found himself blacklisted.

In 1947, Arnold Zander appointed Wurf as an organizer with AFSCME in New York City. Although Zander recognized that Wurf was a rebel, he needed a strong individual to build up AFSCME in New York, and agreed to give Wurf the freedom to do what was necessary, in exchange for personal loyalty.[30]

At the time, the New York local was an ineffectual organization competing with the Teamsters for workers. According to Wurf, AFSCME in New York was a "shit house. It wasn't corrupt, but it bordered on it."[31] After he butted heads with the local leadership and threatened to quit, Zander appointed Wurf as executive director of AFSCME District Council 37, the umbrella group which reigned over the union's New York City locals.

Not surprisingly, Wurf's appointment did not sit well with many AFSCME local leaders who, resenting Wurf's militant approach, defected with their members to the Teamsters. While that left Wurf with only 600 members, he now had the freedom to try a new, more radical approach. He immediately rejected the behind the scenes lobbying that had been favored by the previous union leadership, and adopted confrontational tactics that would transform the public employee labor movement in the decades to come.[32] Wurf realized that unless "public employees won the right to collective bargaining, they would be perpetual supplicants in dealing with government agencies."[33] To help achieve his aims, Wurf brought thousands of workers to a 1954 meeting with mayoral candidate Robert F. Wagner, Jr, son of the senator who had sponsored the National Labor Relations Act (also known as the Wagner Act.) In front of the workers, Wurf put Wagner on the spot, asking if would support dues check off and extend collective bargaining to public workers in New York City if he were elected. Wagner agreed to both points, obtaining AFSCME's support in his election bid. Wagner won the election, and after continued pressure from the union, issued an executive order granting municipal workers the right to collective bargaining and exclusive representation.

That did not end the matter, as the powerful Robert Moses refused to establish grievance procedures for Parks Department employees or meet with AFSCME representatives.[34] Wurf fought back by turning out 3,000 Parks Department workers to surround the department's headquarters, before marching to City Hall. Moses then relented, agreeing to a representation election in which over 90 percent of the workers voted for AFSCME.[35] Through this type of membership mobilization, AFSCME District Council 37 grew to over 25,000 members by the late 1950s.

Wurf then turned his attention to the international union, where a more militant membership was becoming increasingly frustrated with Arnold Zander's conservative approach. By the early 1960s, Zander ruled AFSCME with an iron fist, trusteeing local councils that disagreed with him, consorting with shady characters, and engaging in questionable financial transactions. While Wurf had long been supportive of Zander, and had "worked with him to try to put down the dissidents" over the years, by the 1960s, Wurf had become put off by Zander's version of unionism, in particular, his failure to support militancy.[36] Backed by members who supported a more confrontational approach, Wurf defeated Zander and became president of AFSCME in 1964.

Wurf immediately established a two-pronged strategy to invigorate public employee unionism. The first part was to advocate for a change in the law to give public workers bargaining rights. To make this happen, AFSCME embarked on an ambitious organizing campaign, with unionists fanning out across the country to sign up new members. The second part of Wurf's strategy "was the stick—the strike."[37] If an employer refused to bargain, organizers would call for a strike, with the full support of the international union. The combination of these two powerful strategies created "an organizing blitz not seen in the United States since the unionization of the auto industry in the 1930s, when the United Auto Workers literally seized physical control of plants with sit-down strikes."[38] AFSCME was involved in hundreds of strike situations during this period, standoffs pitting union activists against intransigent public employers backed by anti-worker state laws and employer-friendly judges.

Many of these conflicts were quite intense. For example, in 1974, AFSCME went up against both the police department and the city government in Baltimore. The struggle began on July 1, when 700 sanitation workers who belonged to the AFSCME local began a wildcat strike, upset with a twenty cent per hour wage increase they had been offered.[39] The wildcat strike was endorsed by the international union, and soon spread to other city departments. The striking workers got a big boost on July 11 when over one thousand Baltimore police offers struck in solidarity.[40] The city saw widespread looting during the police strike, with Maryland Governor Marvin Mandel eventually bringing in state troopers to patrol Baltimore's streets.[41] The strike was finally settled on July 15, with the sanitation workers receiving an immediate twenty-five cent per hour increase, and a forty-five cent per hour raise the following year. However, the settlement failed to include amnesty for the leaders of the police union, and as a result, the police chief fired the AFSCME executive board members who had participated in the strike and eliminated dues check off for the police local.[42]

In an editorial in the *Baltimore Sun*, Wurf defended the right of Baltimore's public workers, including the police, to engage in an illegal strike. The problem, according to Wurf, was not striking workers violating the law, but that state law failed to provide an acceptable alternative:

> When the smoke clears and the reprisal issue is finally
> resolved, one fact will remain: it took a 14 day strike by
> sanitation, jail and other blue collar workers and a five
> day action by hundreds of police to get a fair—not a
> generous—salary increase....It's absurd to debate in a
> vacuum whether these workers have a 'right' to strike.[43]

The example of Jerry Wurf and AFSCME shows how pushing for a militant, membership–driven unionism can yield powerful results. Wurf did not wait for an upsurge to happen; instead,
he fought a thirty-year battle with employers—and within his
own union—to make an upsurge possible. The lesson for today's
public employee unionists is the necessity of coming up with a
long-term strategy for the labor movement based on militancy
and solidarity.

Sweeping Aside the "Organizational Residue"

As we saw with Jerry Wurf and AFSCME, one of the painful, yet
necessary consequences of upsurges is that they typically generate
intense conflicts within labor organizations. There are a number
of reasons for this. First, labor upsurges challenge existing ways
of doing business, which current leaders within the organization
are often wedded to. Upsurges also typically require violating restrictive labor laws and challenging authority in ways that established leaders or institutions are not comfortable with. Finally,
upsurges have a level of spontaneity and unpredictability, which
can unnerve cautious labor leaders. As Beverly Silver points out:
"Labor movements that had been widely seen as hopelessly weak

(or even dead) succeed in making major and wide-ranging gains in a short period of time, often through new forms of struggle that sweep aside the 'organizational residue' left by the previous mass upsurge."[44]

The great upsurges of labor history were typically bottom-up affairs—massive explosions of working class activity. While there were countless organizers and organizations shaping these battles, at the core was the self-activity of workers. The problem with today's vertically structured, staff-dominated unions is that they are not built for grassroots activism. Think of the Wisconsin uprising of 2011. The initial protests were driven not by large statewide or national organizations, but by the Teaching Assistants' Association and the Madison chapter of the teachers union. In a true upsurge, so strong is the push from the working class for change that existing organizations are forced to adapt, or perish.

That is what happened in the 1960s, when teachers transformed the AFT and NEA. The teacher rebellion was largely driven by demands for change at the grassroots level, as in state after state, teachers fought within their organizations for a strike-based strategy. As Marjorie Murphy explains in her history of teacher unionism, *Blackboard Unions*:

> The move toward collective bargaining, from roughly the end of postwar teacher militancy in 1952 to the New York City schoolteachers' strike in 1962, can be characterized as a slow, often discouraging, and sometimes extraordinarily frustrating battle of wits between young, dedicated, idealistic organizers and a stubbornly entrenched bureaucracy that was intent on ignoring them.[45]

In the mid-1950s, the American Federation of Teachers was a conservative organization opposed to the strike and favoring backroom lobbying over teacher mobilization. Within the organization, however, a new wave of teacher activists was agitating for change. David Selden, at the time an organizer in the union, had a vision wherein teachers could play a role in not just changing their organization, but in the overall labor movement. Pushing the union over to organizing and eventually a strike-based strategy was a painstaking process, involving a battle for direction within local and state organizations. Ultimately, this new generation of teachers pushed aside the older, more conservative leaders and took over the union.

In the National Education Association, the process was even more extreme. Entering the 1960s, the nation's largest teachers' organization was dominated by administrators, and staunchly opposed to collective bargaining. Reorienting the direction of the organization to striking meant, in many cases, driving out these long-term administrators. In addition, with the rival AFT winning major gains by striking, the NEA was forced to drop its opposition to collective bargaining and strikes. As a result, after not being "involved in a single work stoppage from 1952 to 1963, and none in 1965," by 1966, the NEA "accounted for 80 percent of the teacher strikes" in the United States.[46] Once the AFT adopted the strike as its main weapon, the NEA was faced with a choice—either embrace the new militancy, or die.

In recent times, some labor commentators and self-styled "progressives" have stated that union democracy and local union autonomy are luxuries the labor movement can no longer afford. They instead argue that labor needs to put in place structures which can contend with the power of massive corporations. At some level they are correct, as many local unions have developed into self-perpetuating bureaucracies with little interest in organizing the broader labor movement. However, the proposed solution to this problem, increased bureaucratization, is clearly not the answer.

By almost any measurement, the trade union movement is in worse shape than ever today. Union membership levels are at depths not seen since the early 1900s. Labor's ability to improve workers' lives is also at historic lows. A major study of strike success rates from the 1800s through the 1970s demonstrates that even in the period prior to the passage of the National Labor Relations Act, unions won a surprising number of strikes.[47] The same cannot be said for the contemporary labor movement, as its chief economic weapons have been largely silenced. For the most part, the focus today is on activism and member recruitment, rather than militant theory. Yet ideas matter. Just look at the conservative movement, which launched an ambitious long-term strategy in the 1970s to not just alter immediate policy decisions, but to reshape political thought towards its ideology. Creating the conditions for a labor upsurge will require a similar, long-term, systematic effort, which must at its core confront the current system of labor laws which prevents successful trade union activity.

11. MINORITY UNIONISM

In 2004, Republican Governor Mitch Daniels eliminated legal collective bargaining rights for public workers in Indiana. In subsequent years, lacking the ability to collective bargain, state workers saw the elimination of seniority rights, drastic increases in healthcare premiums, and stagnant wages. Union membership among state workers in Indiana also dropped precipitously, from 16,408 in 2005 to 1,490 in 2011.[1]

In 2011, despite a spirited fight from trade unionists and other groups, Governor Scott Walker and his Republican legislative majority stripped most public workers in Wisconsin of their bargaining rights. And in 2017, elected officials in Iowa, heavily influenced by what had happned six years earlier in Wisconsin, eliminated dues check off and and most topics of bargaining for public workers.[2]

The above are just a few of the many instances of the recent—and potentially, future—attacks on public employee unions. Without collective bargaining rights, and facing stringent conditions for union certification in many states, public employee unions have been left to organize outside the structure of labor law. In many ways, the clock is being set back fifty years, prior to the passage of laws governing collective bargaining and striking for public workers.

With their unions under attack and membership shrinking, one area that should be of particular interest to today's public employee unionists are how their 1960s-era counterparts were able to spur grand change while representing only a small fraction of the workforce. This concept is known as "minority unionism" because the union does not represent a majority of workers. (More recently, some organizers have coined the term "pre-majority unionism" to show that the goal is to eventually gain majority support.) Because of their minority status, union activists of the 1960s and 1970s were required to adopt a creative organizing approach to union power. Rather than relying on government elections or labor law, they had to win victories on the job in order to demonstrate to other workers that unions were worth joining. From their ultimately successful efforts, public employee unionists today can learn what it takes—the militancy and solidarity, especially—to turn their minority unions into majority unions.

A Brief History of Public Employee Minority Unionism

During the 1950s, David Selden, who would go on to become president of the American Federation of Teachers in the late 1960s, was an organizer with the Teachers Guild, a precursor to the United Federation of Teachers. Assigned to collecting membership cards in New York City, Selden would take the subway from school to school, meeting teachers in lunchrooms and explaining to them the benefits of joining the Guild. As he explained, "Despite my frenetic efforts the Guild was only gaining a hundred or so members a year."[3] Unable to demonstrate to his fellow teachers the tangible benefits of unionization, it was difficult for Selden to convince them to sign union cards. "For every three members who joined," Selden noted, "two others were backsliding."[4] Pondering the economics of the type of organizing he was engaged in, Selden concluded that, "At the rate the union was growing, it would take more than a hundred years to enroll a majority of the teachers."[5]

Selden then hit upon the idea of building committees within individual schools to organize around issues of common concern. Rather than attempting to "sell" workers on the abstract benefits of unionization, these committees would fight for specific demands. In 1958, Selden found a potent issue to motivate teachers—the demand for a duty free lunch period. Prior to the unionization wave of the 1960s, teachers were often required to supervise students during their lunch period. Thousands of teachers signed petitions for the union's "Right to Eat" campaign. Seizing the momentum, organizers added wage demands.When the Board of Education failed to come through with a promised wage increase, the union scheduled a one-day work stoppage. Although the strike was averted when the Board of Education found extra money, union membership soared in the wake of this campaign. The union used this momentum to carry out the 1960 teachers' strike, which is widely credited with jumpstarting the teacher rebellion of the 1960s and 1970s. Selden had found that the key to turning a union from minority to majority status was not the tedious and difficult task of convincing individual members to join, but rather collective action around issues that affected everyone.

The previously discussed 1968 strike by sanitation workers in Memphis is another excellent example of the minority union process. While the strike itself is part of labor—and sadly, American—history, what is less known are the tireless efforts of a small group of sanitation workers who organized in obscurity for nearly a decade. Nor is it widely known that the 1968 strike was actually the third sanitation strike in five years in the city of Memphis.

Shortly after being hired in 1959 by Memphis's Department of Public Works, which was in charge of garbage collection, T.O. Jones began agitating among his co-workers for unionization. Jones and a handful of committed organizers worked selflessly to try and build the union. As one account stated, "It took years for that circle of organizers to prepare a base for unionism among rank-and-file workers, and Jones meanwhile lived with great doubt and uncertainly."[6]

Attempts to get the Teamsters involved fizzled after the group's leadership sold out a planned strike in 1960.[7] With little union support, Jones and his men began calling themselves the "Independent Workers Association" and started to put together their own union structure. On June 16, 1963, the group managed to turn out 100 workers to a meeting in a union hall. The mayor of Memphis reacted to this by firing thirty-three presumed leaders of the Independent Workers Association. The workers were eventually rehired, but Jones, undeterred, kept on organizing, "holding secret meetings and talking to individuals one-on-one, trying constantly to get them to pay union dues."[8] Eventually, the group received a union charter from AFSCME president Jerry Wurf. The group, now AFSCME Local 1733, continued as a minority union, with only forty dues paying members out of 1,300 sanitation workers in the city of Memphis.[9]

In February 1968, after two sanitation workers died in a trash compactor due to faulty safety procedures, worker frustration boiled over. According to *At the River I Stand: Memphis, The 1968 Strike and Martin Luther King*, "T.O. Jones called for a special protest meeting of Public Works men that same night. Four to five hundred of them were packed into the Labor Temple meeting hall. Maybe fifty of them were dues paying members of the union. Many had never attended a union meeting before."[10] The workers decided to go on strike, and the rest is history—all because of the tireless efforts of T.O. Jones and a few other men who built the union from the ground up.

To take one more example, while the Professional Air Traffic Controllers Organization (PATCO) is famous for its failed 1981 strike, the growth of the union was actually due to the work of a small group of minority unionists who built what Joseph McCartin describes as "the most militant Federal union."[11] Air traffic controllers were unlikely candidates for militancy, with many being ex-military, with a generally conservative outlook. Yet, as McCartin writes, PATCO was part of a movement in the 1960s of "largely white, uniformed government workers who had not been prone to militancy before, such as police officers and fire fighters."[12] Key to PACTO's development was a series of slowdowns and sickouts spanning the mid-1960s through the late 1970s. In August 1966, air traffic controllers at Chicago's O'Hare Airport, one of the busiest airports in the country, "decided to make use of a time-honored union tactic and began a slowdown to protest pay and working conditions."[13] Although the slowdown was successful, the demands of the controllers were not completely satisfied. Therefore, a year later, in August 1967, the controllers at O'Hare engaged in another slowdown, which won major concessions from management, including an average $1,100 raise.

Upon hearing of the success of their fellow controllers in Chicago, air traffic controllers in Los Angeles engaged in a slowdown of their own, winning job upgrades and improvements in their working conditions.[14] Following that, the flood gates opened, as controllers in other cities began "drawing up their own demands and preparing job actions which could help realize them."[15] All of this activity was done by workers without a nationwide union behind them, without bargaining rights, or a legal right to strike. However, by engaging in these campaigns and winning, union organizers were able to pull others to their cause and form a truly national union.

These examples of minority unionism from the 1960s offer a number of lessons for today's public worker activists. First, the minority union efforts were supported by long-term organizing and agitating based in the workplace. Long before these struggles gained national attention, activists like T.O. Jones and David Selden were pushing and organizing for union recognition. The union was not an outside entity, but something that developed out of workplace struggle.

In addition, these minority unions only gained members when they were able to demonstrate to other workers the tangible benefits of unionization. For many union organizers today, the prize is signing up as many members as possible. However, this does not mean that these members necessarily share common goals or beliefs, or have any understanding of solidarity or militancy. In the 1960s, minority unions grew into majority unions only when they were able to demonstrate the power—through striking or the credible threat thereof—to improve workers' lives. Only a fraction of teachers were union members prior to the 1960 strike; similarly, not many Memphis sanitation workers were paying union dues when they decided to strike in 1968. Air traffic controllers only came to see PATCO as a vehicle for change after a series of successful sickouts and slowdowns. It was power, not membership numbers, that initially made these unions attractive to other workers, and allowed them to eventually grow into large, national organizations.

Minority Unionism Today

With unions on the ropes today, alternative forms of organizing workers have become increasingly popular as a strategy for labor revitalization. These efforts include community-based worker centers, industry-specific forms of workplace organizing such as the Restaurant Opportunities Center, and occupation-specific groups such as the New York City Taxi Drivers Alliance and the farm worker's group, the Coalition of Immokalee Workers. All of these groups represent a minority of workers in a workplace or industry, eschew formal collective bargaining, and rely on alternative sources of labor pressure. Labor writer Josh Eidelson refers to these minority strategies as "alt-labor," because these groups are seen as an alternative to traditional trade unionism.[16]

Worker centers, which have been around since the early 1990s, are efforts to organize low-wage, often immigrant communities which are not represented by unions and/or are excluded from collective bargaining. Frequently funded by non-profits, worker centers have expanded significantly in the last decade and a half as activists have searched for ways to organize groups not reachable by traditional unions. It was not until 2012, however, following a series of one-day strikes by Wal-Mart workers across the country, longer strikes by warehouse workers in Chicago and Los Angeles, and short strikes by restaurant workers in numerous cities, that these non-union organizing efforts really began to be seen as a viable alternative to traditional unionism. In a widely heralded move, the AFL-CIO at its September 2013 convention passed resolutions allowed worker centers and other non-union organizing groups to affiliate with the union federation.[17]

Another area where minority unionism is prevalent today are in "right to work" states which, under the Taft-Hartley Act, are allowed to prohibit union security clauses which require workers to pay for the costs of negotiating agreements and job security provisions. Long-time labor strategists and commentators Rand Wilson and Steve Early write about "the unfolding debate within labor about how best to respond to such daunting open shop conditions" in the increasing number of states which don't provide for collective bargaining or dues check off for public employees.[18]

For many public employees in these—typically southern— "right to work" states, the need to conduct unionism without any type of legal or governmental support is nothing new. As Wilson and Early point out, "[p]ublic sector unionists with long experience in open shop states like Tennessee, Mississippi, North Carolina, or Texas argue that all is not lost for their brothers and sisters north of the Mason-Dixon line."[19] During the 1960s and 1970s, while workers in many northern states won dues check off, exclusive representation, and bargaining with either the right to strike or arbitration, most, but not all, workers in southern states did not gain any formal collective bargaining rights. In the absence of these rights, public workers in the South developed members-only unions, which represented a minority of the workforce. The United Electrical Workers Local 150, for example, has built a strong minority union in North Carolina. In 2013, UE Local 150 won an agreement from the Charlotte city council allowing voluntary dues check off.[20] The union had previously secured such agreements in other North Carolina cities, including Raleigh, Durham and Chapel Hill.[21] Even in the absence of formal bargaining rights, Local 150 has built chapters at public universities and municipalities in North Carolina, winning campaigns over individual terminations, establishing the right of union representatives to attend disciplinary meetings, and helping win pay increases and a grievance procedure for state workers.[22]

Overall, there are a number of significant differences between today's minority union initiatives and similar efforts in the 1960s. Fifty years ago, worker upsurges were very much bottom up affairs, with local union activists fighting within their own organizations for change. In contrast, today's "alt-worker" initiatives are not necessarily led by workers. Many worker centers, for example, receive funding not from employee dues, but from outside foundations, many of which are funded by the very corporate elites unions are fighting against. Steve Early offered up a rare and refreshing critique of the fanfare over the AFL-CIO's actions supporting non-union groups such as Working America, noting that "dumbing down the concept of membership, in the process, is not a 'strategic shift' so much as a shell game. It has little in common with existing serious, long-term efforts to build workplace organization in the absence of employer recognition and bargaining rights."[23] The 1960s era public employee upsurge required intense conflict within unions to transform them into fighting organizations capable of meeting the needs of the existing, and potential, membership.

Furthermore, unions grew in the 1960s through the power of worker self-activity. Many of today's actions, however, are largely created by outside organizations, not workers themselves. None of this is meant to be critical of these outside organizers—quite the opposite. By adopting demonstration strikes, these organizers are reorienting to the workplace and acknowledging that any revival of the labor movement will come from the workers involved. That realization in and of itself is a step forward towards the possibility of a worker upsurge.

In the end, however, it is simply impossible to envision any significant change in the state of the labor movement without a large campaign of civil disobedience and mass defiance of labor laws. The sooner the movement comes to grips with this simple truth, the better. Public employee unionism in the 1960s and 1970s showed that by directly confronting repressive labor law, great things were possible.

CONCLUSION: JANUS, MILITANCY AND THE FUTURE OF PUBLIC EMPLOYEE UNIONISM

In June 2018, the Supreme Court of the United States issued its decision in the case of *Janus v. American Federation of State, County, and Municipal Employees, Council 31*, widely regarded as the most important labor rights decisions in years. Upending four decades of settled law, the Court ruled that agency fee provisions were unconstitutional restrictions on free speech.[1]

Previously, public employee unions had been allowed to charge workers who belonged to the bargaining unit, but who were not members of the union, a percentage of union dues known as "agency fees." However, these fees had to be "germane" to the union's collective bargaining activities, and could not be used for political purposes, such as lobbying for legislation or supporting a candidate.[2]

In *Janus*, Justice Samuel Alito, writing for the Court's 5 to 4 majority ruling in the case, found that the free speech rights of non-union public workers were violated because they were compelled to support union activity, which the Court held constituted free speech. As a result, Alito wrote that union agency agreements violated "the free speech rights of nonmembers by compelling them to subsidize private speech on matters of substantial public concern."[3]

The ruling overturned the Court's 1977 decision in *Abood v. Detroit Board of Education*, in which a group of Detroit teachers had argued that the requirement that they pay fees equivalent to union dues were a violation of their free speech rights. The Court ruled back then that as long as dues collected from non-members was used only for collective bargaining, contract administration, or grievance adjustment, it did not violate the non-members' first amendment rights.

In a decision dripping with contempt for public workers, the Court's right-wing majority took it upon itself to overturn forty years of established law in *Janus*. Alito wrote that although losing the agency fees would place a financial burden on public employee unions—which would have to continue to represent non-members even though they were no longer paying dues—"we must weigh these disadvantages against the considerable windfall that unions have received."[4]

What had changed since 1977? Certainly not the Constitution, or the underlying facts concerning agency fees. Rather, the ideological orientation of the Supreme Court had shifted far to the right. Courts generally follow a doctrine called *stare decisis*, which is the idea that once a legal issue is settled, it should not be overturned. If the Court seesaws back and forth with the passing political winds, it undermines its authority with the public and exposes the political nature of its decision-making. As a result, courts often try to avoid sharp u-turns in policy. But the Supreme Court is now dominated by right wing zealots, a product of decades of conservative efforts to pack the judiciary with anti-union judges, who have no issue overturning what should be settled law to suit their agenda.

Despite their decision in *Janus*, there is little reason to believe that Justice Alito and his fellow conservative Supreme Court justices really believe in the free speech rights of workers. Instead, they used the excuse of the First Amendment to push their conservative political agenda. Justice Elena Kagan, writing the dissent in *Janus*, accused the right-wing majority of "weaponizing" the First Amendment in support of conservative causes, and undemocratically overturning the decisions of elected policymakers. In uncharacteristically harsh language, Kagan called the five justices who ruled in the majority in *Janus* "black-robed rulers overriding citizens' choices." She is also called the justices out for "turning the First Amendment into a sword, and using it against workaday economic and regulatory policy."[5]

In reality, the *Janus* decision was about squelching free speech. Strong unions, and strong public employee unions, promote free speech in an economy dominated by corporate interests. The rise of the public employee movement of the 1960s and 1970s created an organized force which promoted accountability at all levels of government. In direct opposition to this, Justice Alito and the conservative interests on the Supreme Court want to limit democracy and free speech for public workers. If Alito and company really cared about the free speech rights of workers, they would undo the repressive system of labor control which consistently denies such rights to working people. Instead, unions in the private sector are subject to harsh rules and penalties against picketing employers, while federal workers are denied the right to engage in political activity under the anti-union Hatch Act.

Following the *Janus* decision, some in the labor movement suggested that unions abandon the concept of exclusive representation, essentially embracing the new framework established by the Court's ruling. Writing in *In These Times*, labor activists James Gray Pope, Peter Kellman and Ed Bruno called the concept of exclusive representation "dated," further arguing that "[w]e believe it is time to step back, change course and scrap exclusive representation in favor of a system that would let workers join their union of choice."[6]

A general concern of those who propose getting rid of exclusive representation is that unions will be required to pay to represent non-dues paying members without receiving dues income. While on one hand this might make sense—after all, why should union members subsidize non-union members—the idea reflects a narrow, conservative vision of trade unionism. Trade union supporters who urge unions to discard exclusive representation are forgetting their labor history. While they point to problems with the existing system of single employer bargaining and unfair government sponsored elections, rather than embracing a fuller solidarity and militancy, they counsel acceptance of a program favorable to employers. Unionists traditionally set their sights much higher and claimed to represent workers in an entire industry— or even the entire working class. This was true of the relatively conservative American Federation of Labor in the early 1900s, the radical Industrial Workers of the World, and the Congress of Industrial Organizations from the 1930s through the 1970s.

This wasn't just an ideological choice; it was the only way to set industry-wide standards for wages and conditions. Labor rejected the idea that individuals should have the option to undercut the rest of the workers by selling their labor at less than the union rate. Those who crossed picket lines were deplored as scabs. By insisting on a closed shop, which required hiring only union members, unions weren't just securing dues payments—they were challenging management for control of the workplace itself.

Unionists of the 1960s and 1970s also rejected the idea that class struggle was confined to a single enterprise. Instead, they sought to speak for all workers in a given industry, negotiating bargaining agreements that covered a large swath of employees. By the 1950s, major industries such as mining, steel, and trucking had master agreements covering hundreds of thousands of workers. For example, by the late 1960s, 400,000 truck drivers were covered by the Teamster National Master Freight Agreement.

Winning such a contract often required striking against many employers at once, as there is power in numbers. For instance, 500,000 steel workers struck for several months in 1959, crippling industry across the United States and forcing President Eisenhower to intervene. Employers, meanwhile, argued that joining unions, and crossing picket lines, were individual choices. They landed a major blow against solidarity and union power when they outlawed closed shops for private sector workers with the Taft-Hartley Act of 1947.

The agency fee arrangement was labor's fallback in the private sector after Taft-Hartley, a much weaker substitute for the closed shop. Workers could not be required to join unions, but they could be required to pay the cost of certain core representation, such as bargaining and grievance processing. Subsequent Supreme Court decisions even before *Janus* further eroded these fees.

When public employees organized in the 1960s and 1970s, they fell into this framework. To be clear, public workers had to fight and often strike for things like dues checkoff, agency fee arrangements, and exclusive representation. And some public employee unions, including federal worker unions, have never had agency fee protections. But generations of public employee unionists fought for and supported these concepts. Those who say we should ditch exclusive representation are not adopting a radical position that we go back to the pre-compromise position; rather they are suggesting we accept the open shop as the new model for labor relations. Employers have long favored this position; from the open-shop movement of the early 1900s to the anti-union Taft-Hartley Act to opposing public-employee unionism in the 1960s, employers have always rejected the idea that unions represent more than a collection of individual workers. Seen in that light, the *Janus* decision is not simply a hit on dues collection or who contributes for arbitration; what's really in dispute is control of the workplace. Eliminating agency fee provisions is a way to destroy union solidarity. The antidote to *Janus* is not narrowness, but solidarity.

Fortunately, many public employee activists have embraced this approach. Delegates to the 2018 AFSCME International Convention passed a resolution stating that "AFSCME and its affiliates will oppose efforts that undermine the union's status as a democratic, member-run exclusive representative of bargaining."[7] One of the supporters of the resolution, Cherrene Horazuk, longtime President of AFSCME 3800 at the University of Minnesota, explained why this was important:

> The solution is to build the fight, not to hunker down. It is to expand the bonds of solidarity, not narrow them. Instead of looking for every other alternative method, we should focus on the union-building tactics that history has proven are successful: workplace action, strikes, and solidarity.[8]

AFSCME International President Lee Saunders succinctly laid out the union argument against such a narrow approach:

> A union is its members, and a union's strength is derived from the entire workforce speaking out, member and non-member alike. By segregating workers into "us" and "them," unions erode their status and their power. Members-only representation is a short walk away from members-only contracts, which diminish the collective power of the workforce and are inherently divisive and weak.[9]

Luckily the future of the labor movement is not controlled by the Supreme Court. As public employees of the 1960s and 1970s demonstrated, what matters most is not what the courts say, but what the labor movement believes. And despite the war on labor in recent years, as well as some more restrictive voices from inside the movement, there are signs that a newly energized, militant strand of public employee unionism is up for the challenges of today.

The Teacher Rebellion and the Future of American Labor

In the spring of 2018, an incredible grassroots rebellion by thousands of teachers in the Republican-dominated "red" states of West Virginia, Arizona and Oklahoma shook the nation. Fed up with years of underfunding of public education and lagging pay, teachers shut down the public school system in each of these states. Dominating the news cycle and winning widespread support from the public, striking teachers forced conservative politicians to grant them numerous concessions before they would return to work.

In a simultaneous "blue state" rebellion, teachers in several Democratic states struck as well. In the fall of 2018, teachers in Washington State engaged in the most significant strike wave in decades, involving thirteen school districts. In story lines that could have been taken from their 1960's-era forbearers, teachers defied injunctions and won impressive gains, including pay raises ranging from 14 to 19 percent.[10] The teacher strike wave has extended into 2019, with strikes in California, Virginia, Tennessee, South Carolina, and elsewhere.

The parallels between the teacher strike wave and the 1960s and 1970s public worker rebellion are striking, no pun intended. For a labor movement that has long been on the defensive, mired within a repressive labor system, these strikes point the way forward, demonstrating the following:

Strikes Work

Anyone who doubted the continued relevance of the 1960s and 1970s public employee upsurge just needed to see rabid anti-union Republican politicians crumble in the face of striking red state teachers. With thousands of teachers in the streets, politicians chose conciliation and negotiation, setting aside ideology to make these disputes go away.

There is Such Thing as an Illegal Strike, Just an Unsuccessful One

Striking was illegal in each of these states, but that mattered little, as today's conservative politicians face the same dilemma as their predecessors in the 1960s. Certainly, they could have engaged in repressive tactics, but the danger with repression is that it can easily intensify the dispute. For those in the labor movement who see militancy as our only hope, this was good news, showing that the same principals at play in the 1960s and 1970s remain relevant today.

Grassroots Rebellion

Just as in the public employee rebellion of a half century ago, the teacher strike wave was driven by grassroots activities. Organizing through social media and interpersonal networks, striking teachers worked with—and sometimes around—their unions. Just like back in the day.

True Social Unionism

In this book, we have discussed social unionism, in which the demands of public workers fused with the demands of the community to establish powerful movements. In the teacher strike wave, the unrepentant message of funding for public education won over public opinion.

Reviving the Strike

Strike Back, and my previous book, *Reviving the Strike*, were written because the labor movement had abandoned its most effective tool, the strike. In recent years, however, many in labor have again embraced striking as a core component of union strategy. The teacher strike wave demonstrates that the strike is not going away, and can again be a powerful weapon for unions. For as long as workers have worked for wages, they have responded to injustice in the workplace by withholding their labor. That, more than anything, should offer optimism for labor's future. When workers take a notion, great things are indeed possible.

Acknowledgments

I would like to thank all those who supported me in the effort to write this book, including J Berger, Mark Meinster, Jackson Potter, Peter Rachleff and Steve Early.Cherrene Horazak and Ellen David Freeman both read multiple drafts of the book and provided much helpful feedback. I was fortunate to have two leading authorities on the public sector strike, legal historians' Joseph Slater and Joseph McCartin, offer detailed suggestions which greatly improved the manuscript. I was also able to draw extensively on their published work in this under-studied area of labor history. Law professor James Pope, a leading authority on legal restrictions on the right to strike offered many useful suggestions.

Thanks to Elizabeth Clementson and Robert Lasner of Ig Publishing for agreeing to once again publish my work and to Robert for extensive editing which greatly improved the final product.

Over the years, I have been fortunate to work with many great public sector union members. I learned much about unionism from my time as a hospital worker at the University of Minnesota Medical Center and my stint as steward, local union president and member of the statewide AFSCME Council 6 executive board. Negotiating a variety of public sector contracts, and doing strike support on others, allowed me to work with many fine trade unionists and develop first-hand knowledge of the issues involved.

Notes

FOREWORD

1. Burns 2014, 10.
2. Cited in "Attorney General: Teacher Strike is Illegal," wvmetronews. com, February 21, 2018.
3. Joseph Flaherty, "Arizona Schools Chief Diane Douglas Threatens Teachers Over Strike, Says It's 'Not Legal'," *Phoenix New Times*, April 24, 2018. https://www.phoenixnewtimes.com/news/arizona-schools-chief-diane-douglas-threatens-teachers-over-strike-says-its-not-le-gal-10364151
4. Cited in Jake Jarvis, "State Superintendent Reflects on Teacher Strike," wvnews.com, March 14, 2018.
5. Jon Gabriel, "If Arizona Teachers Strike Now, It's a War Against Parents, Not Politicians," *The Arizona Republic*, April 24, 2018.
6. Corey Robin, "Striking Teachers Are 'Real Resistance' to 'Incoherent' Republicans and 'Gutted' Dems," interview by Amy Goodman, Democracy Now!, April 12, 2018.
7. Cited in Lynn Parramore, "The Corporate Plan to Groom U.S. Kids for Servitude by Wiping Out Public Schools," ineteconomics.org, April 6, 2018.

1. THE STRIKE AND THE MAKING OF PUBLIC EMPLOYEE UNIONISM

1. Ben Smith & Maggie Haberman, "Pols Turn on Labor Unions," *Politico*, June 10, 2010, http://www.politico.com/news/stories/0610/38183.html.
2. Pat Garofalo, "Gov. Daniels Bashes Public Employees As 'A New Privileged Class,'" *Think Progress*, June 7, 2010, http://thinkprogress.org/economy/2010/06/07/173307/daniels-public-pay/

3. Joseph A. McCartin, "A Wagner Act for Public Employees: Labor's Deferred Dream and the Rise of Conservatism, 1970-1976," *Journal of American History* (2008): 123.

4. Robert Shaffer, "Where Are the Organized Public Employees? The Absence of Public Employee Unionism from U.S. History Textbooks, and Why It Matters," *Labor History* 43 (2002): 315-334.

5. Joseph McCartin, *Collision Course: Ronald Reagan, The Air Traffic Controllers, and the Strike That Changed America* (Oxford: Oxford University Press, 2011), 103.

6. David Ziskind, *One Thousand Strikes of Government Employees* (New York: Columbia University Press, 1940), 7.

7. Joseph E. Slater, *Public Workers: Government Employee Unions, the Law, and the State, 1900-1962* (Ithaca and London: Cornell University Press, 2004).

8. Richard Kearney, *Labor Relations in the Public Sector, Fourth Edition* (Boca Raton: CRC Press, 2009).

9. Joseph Slater, "Labor and the Boston Police Strike of 1919," in *The Encyclopedia of Strikes in American History*, Aaron Brenner, Benjamin Day and Immanuel Ness, eds. (Armonk: M.E.Sharpe, 2009).

10. Ibid, 243.

11. Ibid, 247.

12. Ibid.

13. Ibid, 246.

14. Ibid, 249.

15. Ibid, 250.

16. Ibid.

17. Cal Thomas, "Time for School Choice in Chicago," *Baltimore Sun*, September 15, 2012 http://articles.baltimoresun.com/2012-09-15/news/bal-time-for-school-choice-in-chicago-20120914_1_school-voucher-voucher-program-voucher-students

18. Jack Stieber, *Public Employee Unionism: Structure, Growth, Policy* (Washington, D.C.: The Brookings Institution, 1973).

19. Slater, *Public Workers: Government Employee Unions, the Law, and the State*, 1900-1962, 74.

20. Ziskind, *One Thousand Strikes of Government Employees*, 139.

21. Ibid, 176-177.

22. Roger V. Seifert, *Teacher Militancy: A History of Teachers Strikes 1896-1987* (London: Falmer Press, 1987), 59.

23. John P. Lloyd, "Strikes, Teachers," in *The Encyclopedia of Strikes in American History*, eds. Aaron Brenner, Benjamin Day and Immanuel Ness (Armonk: M.E. Sharpe, 2009), 254.

24. Seifert, *Teacher Militancy: A History of Teachers Strikes 1896-1987*, 59.

25. Jack Metzgar, "The 1945-1946 Strike Wave," in *The Encyclopedia of Strikes in American History*, 223.

26. Joseph E. Slater, *Public Workers: Government Employee Unions, the Law, and the State, 1900-1962*, 94.

27. Ibid, 94.

28. Dennis Gaffney, *Teachers United: The Rise of New York State United Teachers* (Albany: State University of New York Press, 2007), 33.

29. Joe Burns, *Reviving the Strike: How Working People Can Regain Power and Transform America* (Brooklyn: Ig Publishing, 2011), 12.

30. Immanuel Ness, "Introduction to Pubic Employee Strikes," in *The Encyclopedia of Strikes in American History*, 239.

31. Richard Murphy, "Public Employee Strikes," in *The Crisis in Public Employee Relations in the Decade of the Seventies*, ed. Richard Murphy and Morris Sackman (Washington, DC: Bureau of National Affairs, 1970), 73.

32. Slater, Public Workers: Government Employee Unions, the Law, and the State, 1900-1962, 71.

33. Dane M. Partridge, "A Time Series Analysis of Public Sector Strike Activity," *Journal of Collective Negotiations*, (1991): 3.

34. Ibid, 3.

35. Stieber, *Public Employee Unionism: Structure, Growth, Policy*, 159.

36. Marcus Widenor, "A Small City Police Strike: Klamath Falls, Oregon 1973," *Journal of Collective Negotiations* (1973): 184.

37. Ibid, 187.

38. Ibid, 188.

39. Willian D, Gentel and Martha L Handman, *Police Strikes: Causes and Prevention* (Washington, D.C.: National Institute of Justice,

1980).

40. Ibid, 98.

41. Herbert Northrup and J. Daniel Morgan, "Memphis Police and Firefighters Strikes of 1978: A Case Study," *Labor Law Journal*, January 1981.

42. Steve Early, "CWA Grass Roots Organizing Drive Proves Popular with Jersey Workers," *Labor Notes*, March 1981; Steve Early, "Building a New Public Employee Union," Labor Update, October/November 1982

43. Early, "Building a New Public Employee Union."

44. Shaffer, "Where Are the Organized Public Employees? The Absence of Public Employee Unionism from U.S. History Textbooks, and Why It Matters," 315-334.

45. Arnold M. Zach, "Impasses, Strikes and Resolutions," in *Public Workers and Public Unions*, by The American Assembly, (Englewood Cliffs: Prentice-Hall, 1972), 102.

2. THE TEACHER REBELLION

1. Gaffney, *Teachers United: The Rise of New York State United Teachers*,1.

2. David Selden, *The Teacher Rebellion* (Washington, D.C: Howard University Press, 1985), 10.

3. Gaffney, *Teachers United: The Rise of New York State United Teachers*, 25.

4. Ibid, 26.

5. Lloyd, "Strikes,Teachers," 255.

6. Gaffney, *Teachers United: The Rise of New York State United Teachers*, 27.

7. Ibid, 38.

8. Lloyd, "Strikes, Teachers," 256.

9. Murphy, "Public Employee Strikes," 74.

10. Sterling Spero and John Capozzola, *The Urban Community and Its Unionized Bureaucracies* (New York: Dunellen, 1973,) 247.

11. Selden, *The Teacher Rebellion*, 109.

12. Spero and Capozzola, *The Urban Community and Its Unionized Bureaucracies*, 248.

13. Partridge, "A Time Series Analysis of Public Sector Strike Activity," 4.

14. Seifert, *Teacher Militancy: A History of Teachers Strikes 1896-1987*, 99.

15. Lloyd, "Strikes, Teachers," 256.

16. Harold Selig Roberts, *Labor Relations in the Public Sector* (University of Hawaii Press, 1970), 433.

17. Steve Kink and John Cahill, *Class Wars: The Story of the Washington Education Association 1965—2001* (Seattle: Washington Education Association, 2004), 43.

18. Marjorie Murphy, *Blackboard Unions: The AFT and the NEA 1900-1980* (Ithaca: Cornell University Press, 1990), 209.

19. Kink and Cahill, *Class Wars: The Story of the Washington Education Association 1965-2001*, 2.

20. Ibid, 30.

21. Ibid, 59.

22. Ibid, 74.

23. Ibid, 76.

24. "School Survey Postponed Again," *Chicago Tribune*, March 14 1963: B.2.

25. "Strike Vote is Withheld by Teachers," *Chicago Tribune*, Feb 27, 1964.

26. "Picket Signs Pay Off for Teachers," *Chicago Tribune*, June 5, 1967, 14.

27. BobboSphere, "Educational apartheid in Chicago and the black teachers revolt of the 1960s," Daily Kos, October 25, 2012, http://www.dailykos.com/story/2012/10/25/1149692/-Educational-apartheid-in-Chicago-the-black-teachers-revolt-of-the-1960-s

28. Ibid.

29. Stephen Pratt, "Teachers Make Threats Pay with 90% Pay Hikes Since 1966," *Chicago Tribune*, September 26, 1974, S4.

30. Andrea Johnson, "Minot teachers go on strike in 1969", *Minot Daily News*, October 1, 2008 http://www.minotdailynews.com/page/content.detail/id/519525.html?nav=5576

31. Hortonville School District v. Hortonville Education Association,

482 U.S. (1976).

32. Wisconsin Education Association Council, "WEAC History Book Chapter," http://www.weac.org/about_weac/history/history_book_chp5-1.aspx>

33. Stephanie Simon, "Teacher Unions Face Moment of Truth," *Politico*, December 8, 2013, http://www.politico.com/story/2013/12/education-teachers-unions-moment-of-truth-national-education-association-american-federation-of-teachers-100813.html

34. Henry A. Giroux, "Can Democratic Education Survive in a Neoliberal Society?" Truthout, October 16, 2012, http://truth-out.org/opinion/item/12126-can-democratic-education-survive-in-a-neoliberal-society

35. Doug Henwood and Liza Featherstone, "Marketing Schools," *Monthly Review Press* 65, no. 2 (June 2013) http://monthlyreview.org/2013/06/01/marketizing-schools

36. Lois Weiner, "Privatizing Public Education: The Neoliberal Model," *New Political Spaces* 19, no. 1 (2012) http://reimaginerpe.org/19-1/weiner

37. Murphy, *Blackboard Unions: The AFT and the NEA 1900-1980*, 209.

3. THE BACKLASH AGAINST PUBLIC EMPLOYEE UNIONISM AND THE DECLINE OF THE STRIKE

1. Joseph McCartin, "Fire the Hell Out of Them: Sanitation Workers' Struggles and the Normalization of the Striker Replacement Strategy in the 1970s." *Labor: Studies in Working-Class History of the Americas* (2005): 67-92, 79.

2. Joseph Goulden, *Jerry Wurf: Labor's Last Angry Man* (New York: Atheneum, 1982), 240.

3. Ibid, 240.

4. McCartin, "Fire the Hell out of Them: Sanitation Workers' Struggles and the Normalization of the Striker Replacement Strategy in the 1970s."

5. Ibid, 77.

6. Ibid, 80.

7. Ibid, 86-87.

8. Ibid, 90.

9. Joseph McCartin, *Collision Course: Ronald Reagan, The Air Traffic Controllers, and the Strike that Changed America* (Oxford: Oxford University Press, 2011),145.

10. Ibid, 206.

11. Ibid, 262.

12. Richard Kearney, *Labor Relations in the Public Sector, 3rd Edition* (New York: Marchel Dekker, 2001), 226.

13. Ibid, 225.

14. Joseph Slater, "The Assault on Collective Bargaining: Real Harms and Imaginary Benefits," Unpublished Paper, 2012.

15. Joyce Najita and James Stern, "Introduction and Overview" in *Collective Bargaining in the Public Sector: The Experience of Eight States*, Joyce Najita and James Stern, eds. (Armonk, ME Sharpe, 2001), 5.

16. McCartin, *Collision Course: Ronald Reagan, The Air Traffic Controllers, and the Strike that Changed America*, 214.

17. Jane Mayer, "Covert Operations: The billionaire brothers who are waging a war against Obama," *New Yorker*, August 30, 2010.

18. Barry Hirsch and David Macpherson, "Union Membership and Coverage Database from the CPS," http://www. unionstats.com

19. Richard Hurd and Sharon Pinnock, "Public Sector Unions: Will They Thrive or Struggle to Survive?" *Journal of Labor Research*, 25, no. 2 (2004): 211-221 http://digitalcommons.ilr.cornell.edu/cgi/viewcontent.cgi?article=1893&context=articles

20. Joseph Slater, "The Assault on Collective Bargaining: Real Harms and Imaginary Benefits," Unpublished Paper, 2012.

21. Joe Davidson, "Trump, blocked by court on executive orders, ramps up agency moves against unions," *Washington Post*, July 9, 2019

22. Daniel DiSalvo, "Public-Sector Unions After *Janus*: An Update," The Manhattan Institute, February 14, 2019. https://www.manhattan-institute.org/public-sector-unions-after-janus

4. PUBLIC EMPLOYEE SOCIAL UNIONISM

1. Harry H. Wellington and Ralph R Winter, *The Unions and the Cities* (Washington, DC: The Brookings Institution, 1971), 25-26.

2. Martin Malin, "Public Employees' Rights to Strike: Law and Experience," *University of Michigan Journal of Law Reform* 26, no. 2 (1993): 313, http://works.bepress.com/cgi/viewcontent.cgi?article=1020&context=martin_malin

3. Ibid.

4. Paul Johnston, *Success While Others Fail: Social Unionism in the Public Workplace* (Ithaca: ILR Press, 1994), 12-13.

5. McCartin, "Fire the Hell out of Them: Sanitation Workers' Struggles and the Normalization of the Striker Replacement Strategy in the 1970s," 82

6. Johnston, *Success While Others Fail: Social Unionism in the Public Workplace*, 37.

7. Ibid, 38.

8. Ibid, 37.

9. Ibid, 40.

10. Ibid, 41.

11. Ibid, 43.

12. Ibid, 43.

13. Mark H. Maier, *City Unions: Managing Discontent in New York City* (New Brunswick: Rutgers University Press, 1987), 57.

14. Emmanuel Perlmutter, "City Invokes Law and Ousts 5,398 In Welfare Tie-Up," *New York Times*, January 6, 1965.

15. Sydney Schanberg, "Welfare Strike is Unresolved: Union Chiefs Cheered in Jail," *New York Times*, January 23, 1965; Emmnauel Perlmutter, "16 More Go to Jail in Welfare Tie-Up," *New York Times,* January 26, 1965.

16. Douglas Robinson, "Social Work Pact Signed By Mayor," *New York Times*, June 5, 1965.

17. Mark Maier, *City Unions* (New Brunswick: Rutgers University Press, 1987), 65.

18. "The 1965 New York City Welfare Strike and Worker-Client Alliances," May 19, 2012, http://www.rankandfiler.net/nyc-welfare-strike/

19. Emmanuel Perlmutter, "City to Stop Pay In Welfare Sit-In," *New York Times*, June 19, 1967.

20. "The 1965 New York City Welfare Strike and Worker-Client Alliances."

21. Stieber, *Public Employee Unionism: Structure, Growth, Policy*, 163.

22. James Wooten, "Racial Overtones Mark Strike of Charleston Hospital Workers," *New York Times*, April 5, 1969.

23. James Wooten, "Charleston Port May Face Strike," *New York Times*, June 26, 1969: 24.

24. Jerald E. Podair, *The Strike that Changed New York: Blacks, Whites and the Ocean Hill-Brownsville Crisis* (New Haven: Yale University Press, 2002).

25. Eric Scheiner, "Taking the Public Out of Determining Government Policy: The Need for an Appropriate Scope of Bargaining Test in the Illinois Public Sector," *John Marshall Law Review*, 29 no. 531 (1996).

26. Illinois Educational Labor Relations Act, 115 ILCS 5.

27. Lois Weiner, *The Future of Our Schools: Teacher Unions and Social Justice* (Chicago: Haymarket Books, 2012.)

28. Abby Rapoport, "Labor's Plan B," *The American Prospect*, May 13, 2013, http://prospect.org/article/labors-plan-b

5. THE INSIDE STRATEGY

1. Ronald W Glass, "Work Stoppages and Teachers: History and Prospects," *Monthly Labor Review*, August 1967, 43.

2. Kearney, *Labor Relations in the Public Sector*, 38.

3. Mathew DeFour, "Two Thirds of Madison Teachers Joined Protests—District Says," *Wisconsin State Journal*, April 29, 2011, http://host.madison.com/news/local/govt-and-politics/two-thirds-of-madison-teachers-joined-protests-district-says/article_86781fb4-7288-11e0-92c8-001cc4c03286.html

4. Maier, City Unions: Managing Discontent in New York City, 98.

5. Arthur W. O'Shea, "Detroit Led Way for Police Unions," *The Milwaukee Journal*, January 24, 1971: 11.

6. Police Association of New Orleans, accessed 12/31/2013, http://www.pano1544.com/history.html

7. Maier, *City Unions: Managing Discontent in New York City*, 103.

8. McCartin, *Collision Course: Ronald Reagan, The Air Traffic Controllers, and the Strike that Changed America.*

9. Police Benevolent Asso. v. New York State Public Employment Relations Board, 51 N.Y.2d 779 (N.Y. 1980)

10. Jane Prendergast, "Chief: Fire some 'blue flu' Cops," Cincinnatti.com, Aug. 11, 2009, http://archive.cincinnati.com/article/20090811/NEWS0108/308110036/Chief-Fire-some-blue-flu-cops

11. Jim Provance, "State panel rules Toledo police 'blue flu' was not a strike," *Toledo Blade*, April 8, 2010.

12. Paul Staudohar, "Quasi-Strikes by Public Employees." *Journal of Collective Negotiations*, (1974): 364.

13. Maier, *City Unions: Managing Discontent in New York City*, 95.

14. Ibid, 98.

15. Ibid, 102.

16. Ralph de Toledano, *Let Our Cities Burn* (New Rochelle: Arlington House Publishers, 1975), 45.

17. Stieber, *Public Employee Unionism: Structure, Growth, Policy*, 182.

18. Maier, *City Unions: Managing Discontent in New York City*, 71.

19. Lloyd, "Strikes, Teachers," 264.

20. *Daily News*, "Monday is 'Human Error Day," June 1, 1979.

21. "Mass Resignations by Public School Teachers," 55 Iowa L. Rev. 497 (1969-1970).

22. Berkely Miller and William Canak, "From 'Porkchoppers' to 'Lambchoppers': the Passage of Florida's Public Employees Labor Relations Act," *Industrial and Labor Relations Review* (1991): 356.

23. Don Cameron, *Educational Conflict in the Sunshine State: The Story of the 1968 Statewide Teacher Walkout in Florida* (Lanham: Rowman and Littlefield Education, 2008), 37.

24. Kink and Cahill, *Class Wars: The Story of the Washington Education Association 1965-2001*, 12.

25. Staudohar, "Quasi-Strikes by Public Employees."

26. "Mass Resignations by Public School Teachers," 498.

27. Glass, "Work Stoppages and Teachers: History and Prospects," 43.

28. Miller and Canak, "From 'Porkchoppers' to 'Lambchoppers': the Passage of Florida's Public Employees Labor Relations Act," 356.

29. Ibid, 356.

30. Ibid, 357.

31. Edwin Pendleton and Paul Staudohar, "Arbitration and Strikes in Hawaii Public Employment," *Industrial Relations: A Journal of Economy and Society* (1974): 304.

32. Kink and Cahill, *Class Wars: The Story of the Washington Education Association 1965-2001*, 177.

33. Ibid, 168.

34. Ibid, 168.

35. Ibid, 169.

36. Jane Slaughter and Mark Brenner, "In the Wake of Wisconsin: What Next?" in *Wisconsin Uprising: Labor Fight Back*, Michael Yates, ed. (New York: Monthly Review Press, 2012.)

37. Stieber, *Public Employee Unionism: Structure, Growth, Policy*, 163.

38. Ann Montague, "Nine Days That Shook Oregon Or: How OPEU Became a Union," Labor Standard, accessed December 31, 2013, http://www.laborstandard.org/Nine_Days_That_Shook_Oregon.html.

39. Dan La Botx, "A Troublemaker's Handbook," *Labor Notes* (1991): 81-84.

40. Montague, "Nine Days That Shook Oregon Or: How OPEU Became a Union."

41. La Botx, "A Troublemaker's Handbook."

6. PUBLIC EMPLOYEE BARGAINING AND THE RIGHT TO STRIKE

1. Slater, *Public Workers: Government Employee Unions, the Law, and the State, 1900-1962*, 73.

2. Kearney, *Labor Relations in the Public Sector, Fourth Edition*, 227.

3. Leo Troy, *The New Unionism in the New Society: Public Sector Unions in the Redistributive State* (Fairfax, VA: George Mason University Press, 1994), 79.

4. Slater, *Public Workers: Government Employee Unions, the Law, and the State, 1900-1962*, 79.

5. Cleveland v. Division 268 of Amal. Ass'n 90 N.E.2d 711, 715 (1949).

6. County Sanitation Dist. No. 2 v. Los Angeles County Employees'

Assn., 38 Cal. 3d 564 (Cal. 1985).

7. Dave Jamieson, "Toll Road Privatization: As Ohio Considers It, Indiana Serves As Cautionary Tale," *Huffington Post*, June 16, 2011, http://www.huffingtonpost.com/2011/06/16/toll-road-privatization_n_878169.html

8. Ibid.

9. Mick Dumke and Ben Joravsky, "How Mayor Emanuel locked the parking meter deal in place," *Chicago Reader*, June 6, 2013; Chris Fusco and Dan Mihalopoulos, "Former Mayor Daley's staff saw parking-meter problems brewing, records show," *Chicago Sun Times*, May 22, 2013

10. Daniel DiSalvo, Government Unions and the Bankrupting of America (Encounter Books, 2011.)

11. Mallory Factor and Elizabeth Factor, *Shadowbosses: Government Unions Control America and Rob Taxpayers Blind* (Center Street, 2013), xiv.

12. Daniel DiSalvo, "The Trouble with Public Sector Unions," *National Affairs*, no. 5, 2010, http://www.nationalaffairs.com/publications/detail/the-trouble-with-public-sector-unions

13. Jonathan Salant, "Koch Funneled $1.2 Million to Governors Battling Unions," *Bloomberg News*, February 23, 2011, http://www.bloomberg.com/news/2011-02-23/koch-funneled-1-2-million-to-elect-governors-battling-unions.html

14. Ron Seely, "Walker administration still intends to sell state power plants," *Wisconsin State Journal*, March 19, 2011, http://host.madison.com/news/local/govt-and-politics/walker-administration-still-intends-to-sell-state-power-plants/article_c7c57cc8-51b3-11e0-a99f-001cc4c03286.html

15. Factor and Factor, *Shadowbosses: Government Unions Control America and Rob Taxpayers Blind*.

16. Daniel Bice, "Membership in Public Worker Unions Takes a Hit Under Act 10," *Milwaukee Journal Sentinel*, July 20, 2013, http://www.jsonline.com/watchdog/noquarter/216309111.html

17. Kearney, *Labor Relations in the Public Sector, Fourth Edition*, 228.

18. DiSalvo, "The Trouble with Public Sector Unions."

19. Ibid.
20. County Sanitation Dist. No. 2 v. Los Angeles County Employees' Assn., 38 Cal. 3d 564 (Cal. 1985).
21. Ibid.
22. Ibid.
23. Bruce E. Kaufman, "Historical Insights: The Early Institutionalists on Trade Unionism and Labor Policy," in *What Do Unions Do: A Twenty Year Perspective, Bennett, James and Bruce Kaufman*, eds. (New Brunswick: Transaction Publishers, 2008), 62.
24. "Ellison Calls on President Obama to Require Federal Contractors to Pay a Living Wage," September 26, 2013, http://ellison.house. gov/media-center/press-releases/ellison-calls-on-president-obama-to-require-federal-contractors-to-pay-a
25. Laura Clawson, "Wisconsin Gov. Walker: 'Collective bargaining is not a right.' Actually, Scott, it is," Daily Kos, April 04, 2012, http:// www.dailykos.com/story/2012/04/04/1080531/-Wisconsin-Gov-Walker-Collective-bargaining-is-not-a-right-Actually-Scott-it-is
26. Sper and Capozzola, *The Urban Community and Its Unionized Bureaucracies*, 244.
27. John Samuelsen, "Public Employees Need the Right To Strike," *Labor Notes*, January 4, 2012.
28. Eric Hobsbawm, *Worlds of Labor* (New York: Pantheon Books, 1984), 298.
29. Ibid, 297.
30. 29 U.S. Code § 151, et. seq.
31. NLRB v. Jones & Laughlin Steel Corp., 301 U.S. 1, (1937), 33.
32. Ronald Kahlenberg and Richard D. and Moshe Z. Marvitt, *Why Labor Organizing Should be a Civil Right* (The Century Foundation, 2012.)
33. Jay Youngdahl, "Should labor defend worker rights as human rights? A debate," *New Labor Forum*, 2009, 31-37.
34. Rowland Harvey, *Samuel Gompers: Champion of the Toiling Masses* (California: Stanford University Press, 1935), 45.
35. County Sanitation Dist. No. 2 v. Los Angeles County Employees' Assn., 38 Cal. 3d 564 (Cal. 1985).

36. "As Unions Decline, Inequality Rises," *Economic Policy Institute*, June 6, 2012, http://www.epi.org/publication/unions-decline-inequality-rises/

37. James Pope, "The Right to Strike Under the United States Constitution: Theory, Practice, and Possible Implications for Canada," 2009, http://www.law.utoronto.ca/documents/conferences2/StrikeSymposium09_Pope.pdf.

38. Ibid.

39. Ibid.

40. "Should Your Teacher Strike? (Or Your Mailman? Fireman? Sanitation man? Policeman?)," *American Federation of Teachers*, May 1970, http://www.substancenews.net/articles.php?page=3423.

41. James Gray Pope, "Labor and the Constitution: From Abolition to Deindustrialization," *Texas Law Review*, 65: 1071.

7. PRIVATIZATION AND THE "FREE MARKET"

1. Robert Jay Dilger, Randolph R. Moffett and Linda Struyk, "Privatization of Municipal Services in America's Largest Cities," *Public Administration Review* 57 no. 1 (January/February 1997).

2. Jeffrey Keefe, "Public Employee Compensation and the Efficacy of Privatization Alternatives in US State and Local Governments," *British Journal of Industrial Relations*, 50 no. 4 (December 2012): 782-809

3. Glen Howatt, "Fairview University Medical Center : `Ground rules' for merger signed," *Star Tribune*, January 7, 1997: 3b

4. John Kamensky, "A Brief History," National Partnership for Reinventing Government, http://govinfo.library.unt.edu/npr/whoweare/history2.html

5. Richard Hurd, "In defense of public service: Union strategy in transition," 2003, http://digitalcommons.ilr.cornell.edu/articles/300/

6. Paul Light, "The Real Crisis in Government," *Washington Post*, January 2, 2010, http://www.washingtonpost.com/wp-dyn/content/article/2010/01/11/AR2010011103255.html

7. Hurd, "In defense of public service: Union strategy in transition."

8. "Bad Business: Billions of Taxpayer Dollars Wasted on Hiring Con-

tractors," Project on Government Oversite, 2011, http://www.pogo.org/our-work/reports/2011/co-gp-20110913.html

9. Hurd, "In defense of public service: Union strategy in transition."

10. "Bad Business: Billions of Taxpayer Dollars Wasted on Hiring Contractors,"

11. Moshe Schwartz and Jennifer Church, "Department of Defense's Use of Contractors to Support Military Operations: Background, Analysis, and Issues for Congress," 2013, http://www.fas.org/sgp/crs/natsec/R43074.pdf

12. "Predatory Privatization, Enriching the 1%, Undermining Democracy," People for the American Way, 2012, http://site.pfaw.org/pdf/Predatory-Privatization.pdf

13. Ibid.

14. Diane Rativich, *Reign of Error: The Hoax of the Privatization Movement and the Danger to America's Public Schools* (New York: Alfred Publishing Co., 2013.)

15. "Union affiliation of employed wage and salary workers by occupation and industry," Bureau of Labor Statistics, accessed January 4, 2014, http://www.bls.gov/news.release/union2.t03.htm#union_a03.f.1

16. Talia Milgrom-Elcott, "Unionized Charter Schools: An Unlikely Course Our Democracy Depends On," *Forbes*, May 21, 2019. https://www.forbes.com/sites/taliamilgromelcott/2019/05/21/unionized-charter-schools-an-unlikely-course-our-democracy-depends-on/#43ea7e791cf1

17. Rativich, *Reign of Error: The Hoax of the Privatization Movement and the Danger to America's Public Schools*, Chapter 16.

18. "Predatory Privatization, Enriching the 1%, Undermining Democracy."

19. Ibid.

20. Michael Brickner and Shakyra Diaz, "Prisons for Profit Incarceration for Sale," *Human Rights* 38, no. 3 (Summer 2011): 14-17.

21. Tracy Chang and Douglas Thompkins, "Corporations Go to Prisons: The Expansion of Corporate Power in the Correctional Industry" *Labor Studies Journal* 27, no. 1 (Spring 2002); Brickner Diaz,

"Prisons for Profit Incarceration for Sale."

22. Brickner Diaz, "Prisons for Profit Incarceration for Sale."

23. Emily Smith, "Pennsylvania Judge Mark Ciavarella Sentenced To 28 Years In Prison For Selling Children," May 3, 2013, http://www.opposingviews.com/i/society/crime/pennsylvania-judge-mark-ciavarella-sentenced-28-years-prison-selling-children

24. "Predatory Privatization, Enriching the 1%, Undermining Democracy."

25. Ibid.

26. Anthony Cody, "Prisons, Post Offices and Public Schools: Some Things Should Not Be For Profit," *Education Week*, August 18, 2013, http://blogs.edweek.org/teachers/living-in dialogue/2013/08/prisons_post_offices_and_publi.html?cmp=SOC-SHR-FB

27. Hurd, "In defense of public service: Union strategy in transition."

28. Alex Marshall, *The Surprising Design of Market Economics* (Austin: University of Texas Press, 2012), 19.

29. Ibid.

30. Ibid, 21.

31. Michael J. Sandel, *What Money Can't Buy: The Moral Limits of Markets* (New York: Farrar, Straus and Giroux, 2012), 3.

32. Ibid, 6.

33. Ibid, 7.

8. STRIKING AND THE LAW

1. Kearney, *Labor Relations in the Public Sector, Fourth Edition*, 232.

2. Spero and Capozzola, *The Urban Community and Its Unionized Bureaucracies*, 243.

3. Ibid, 242.

4. Stieber, *Public Employee Unionism: Structure, Growth, Policy*, 116.

5. Ziskind, *One Thousand Strikes of Goverment Employees*, 7.

6. Bernard Yabroff and Mary David Lily, " Collective Bargaining and Work Stoppages Involving Teachers," *Monthly Labor Review*, (May 1953): 475.

7. Ibid, 477.

8. Spero and Capozzola, *The Urban Community and Its Unionized Bu-*

reaucracies, 244.

9. Ibid, 245.

10. Stieber, *Public Employee Unionism: Structure, Growth, Policy*, 178.

11. Ibid, 178-179.

12. Ibid, 179.

13. Ibid, 182.

14. de Toledano, *Let Our Cities Burn*, 44.

15. Malin, "Public Employees Right to Strike: Law and Experience" 360.

16. Paul Staudohar, "The Emergence of Hawaii's Public Employment Law," *Industrial Relations: A Journal of Economy and Society*, 1973, 340.

17. Ibid, 341-342.

18. Ibid, 347-348.

19. Ibid, 348.

20. Corinne Adams Robinson, *The 1970 Minneapolis Teachers Strike* (Minneapolis: Minneapolis Federation of Teachers, 1995), 3.

21. Ibid, 2.

22. Ibid, 9.

23. Malin, "Public Employees Right to Strike: Law and Experience."

24. Carl Ryan, "Mayhem followed 1979 walkout," T*oledo Blade*, April 7, 2010: A.3.

25. Tom Troy, "Bargaining's last overhaul in 1983," *Toledo Blade*, February 18, 2011, http://www.toledoblade.com/local/2011/02/18/Bargaining-last-overhaul-in-1983.html

26. Kearney, *Labor Relations in the Public Sector, Fourth Edition*, 236.

27. Ibid, 236.

28. Cebulski, "An Analysis of 22 Illegal Strikes and California Law," in J. Grodin, and D. Wollet, eds., Labor Relations and Social Problems, A Course Book, Unit Four, Collective Bargaining in Public Employment (Washington DC: BNA, 1975), 246.

29. J. Tomkiewicz, C. Tomkeiwiecz, and O. Brenner. "Why Don't Teachers Strike?" *Journal of Collective Negotiations* (1985): 183.

30. Malin, Public Employees Right to Strike: Law and Experience," 372-373.

31. Ibid, 360.

32. Ibid, 330.

33. Ibid, 333

34. Joseph A. McCartin, "Context Matters More: A Response to Joe Burns," *Labor Studies Journal* 37, no. 4 (2013): 349–352.

9. CHALLENGING UNJUST LABOR LAWS

1. Barry Hirsch and David Macpherson, "Union Membership and Coverage Database from the CPS," http://www. unionstats.com.

2. Robert E. Scott, Carlos Salas, and Bruce Campbell, "Revisiting NAFTA: Still Not Working for North America's Workers," Economic Policy Institute, Briefing Paper 173, September 28, 2006. http://www.epi.org/publication/bp173/

3. Kamensky, "A Brief History."

4. Alexia Fernández Campbell, "A record number of US workers went on strike in 2018." Vox, February 13, 2019. https://www.vox.com/policy-and-politics/2019/2/13/18223211/worker-teacher-strikes-2018-record

5. Chris Rhomberg, *The Broken Table: The Detroit Newspaper Strike and the State of American Labor* (New York: Russell Sage Foundation, 2012), 259-283.

6. Ibid, 276.

7. "The history of the Taylor law," United Federation of Teachers, June 9, 2005. http://www.uft.org/labor-spotlight/history-taylor-law

8. "Labor Law: Stopping Public Employee Strikes," *Time*, January 14, 1966.

9. Wellington and Winter, *The Unions and the Cities*, 186.

10. Theodore W. Kheel, "Strikes and Public Employment," *Michigan Law Review* 67 (1969): 931, 936.

11. Jacques Steinberg, "David Selden, 83, Union Chief Jailed During Teachers Strike" *New York Times*, May 13, 1998.

12. Frances Fox Piven and Richard Cloward, *Poor People's Movements: Why They Succeed, How They Fail*, (New York, Pantheon, 1977), 29.

13. Wellington and Winter, *The Unions and the Cities*, 186.

14. Wayne King, "End of a Bitter Strike: Philadelphia Education," *New*

York Times, (March 4, 1973).

15. Ibid.

16. *Kink and Cahill, Class Wars: The Story of the Washington Education Association 1965-2001*, 66.

17. Ibid, 67.

18. Ibid, 68.

19. Ibid, 69.

20. Ibid, 70.

21. Ibid, 70.

22. Goulden, *Jerry Wurf: Labor's Last Angry Man*, 119.

23. Aaron Brenner, "Postal Workers' Strikes," in *The Encyclopedia of Strikes in American History*, Aaron Brenner, Benjamin Day and Immanuel Ness, eds. (Armonk: M.E.Sharpe, 2009), 266.

24. Philip Rubio, *There's Always Work at the Post Office*, (Chapel Hill: University of North Carolina Press, 2010).

25. Brenner. "Postal Workers' Strikes," 270.

26. Ibid.

27. "The Strike That Stunned the Country" *Time*, 95 no. 13, March 30, 1970, http://content.time.com/time/magazine/article/0,9171,942202,00.html

28. Brenner, "Postal Workers' Strikes," 272-273.

29. "The Strike That Stunned The Country."

30. Brenner, "Postal Workers' Strikes," 276.

31. Piven and Cloward, *Poor People's Movements: Why They Succeed, How They Fail*, 29.

32. Ibid, 29.

33. Wellington and Winter, *The Unions and the Cities*, 187.

34. Goulden, *Jerry Wurf: Labor's Last Angry Man*, 146.

35. Michael K. Honey, *Going Down Jericho Road: The Memphis Strike, Martin Luther King's Last Campaign* (New York: W.W. Norton and Co., 2007), 74.

36. Joan Turner Beifuss, *At the River I Stand, Memphis, The 1968 Strike and Martin Luther King* (Brooklyn: Carlson Publishing, 1985), 110.

37. Gaffney, Teachers United: The Rise of New York State United Teachers, 39.

38. David Ford, Should We Jail Public Employees? (New York: Workers Defense League, 1973.)

39. James O. Morris, *Conflict Within the AFL: A Study of Craft versus Indistrial Unionism, 1901-1938* (Westport, Connecticut: Greenwood Press, 1974),163.

40. Rich Yeselson, "Fortress Unionism," *Democracy: A Journal of Ideas*, no. 29 (Summer 2013), http://www.democracyjournal.org/29/fortress-unionism.php.

10. UPSURGE

1. Dan Clawson, *The Next Upsurge: Labor and the New Social Movements* (Ithaca: ILR Press, 2003), 13.

2. Ibid, 16.

3. Shaffer, "Where Are the Organized Public Employees? The Absence of Public Employee Unionism from U.S. History Textbooks, and Why It Matters."

4. Melvin W. Reder, "The Rise and Fall of Unions: The Public Sector and the Private," *Journal of Economic Perspectives* (1988): 106.

5. Clawon, *The Next Upsurge: Labor and the New Social Movements*, 13.

6. Piven and Cloward, *Poor People's Movements: Why They Succeed, How They Fail.*

7. Philip S. Foner, *History of the Labor Movement in the United States: Postwar Struggles 191-1920* (International Publishers, 1988); Jack Metzgar, "The 1945-1946 Strike Wave," in *The Encyclopedia of Strikes in American History.*

8. Beverly J. Silver, *Forces of Labor: Workers' Movements and Globalization Since 1870* (Cambridge: Cambridge University Press, 2003).

9. Kim Moody, "General Strikes, Mass Strikes," Solidarity Webzine, http://www.solidarity-us.org/site/node/3679.

10. Ibid.

11. Steven Verburg, "Labor group for a general strike if budget bill is approved," *Wisconsin State Journal*, February 23, 2011, http://host.madison.com/news/local/govt-and-politics/labor-group-calls-for-general-strike-if-budget-bill-is/article_64c8d7a8-3e8c-11e0-9911-001cc4c002e0.html

12. Cal Winslow, "Who's Speaking for Whom?: The Case of Occupy and the Longshoremen's Union," *Counterpunch*, December 5, 2011, http://www.counterpunch.org/2011/12/05/the-case-of-occupy-and-the-longshoremen%E2%80%99s-union/

13. Piven and Cloward, *Poor People's Movements: Why They Succeed, How They Fail.*

14. Ibid.

15. Ibid.

16. Ibid.

17. Roger V. Seifert, *Teacher Militancy: A History of Teachers Strikes 1896-1987* (London: Falmer Press, 1987), 59.

18. Ibid, 60.

19. Ibid, 92.

20. Joseph A McCartin, "Unexpected Convergence: Values, Assumptions, and the Right to Strike in Public and Private Sectors, 1945-2005," *Buffalo Law Review* 57, no. 3 (May 2009): 727, 735.

21. Ibid, 727, 734.

22. Spero and Capozzola, *The Urban Community and Its Unionized Bureaucracies*, 244.

23. Arnold M Zach, "Impasses, Strikes and Resolutions," in *Public Workers and Public Unions* (Englewood Cliffs: Prentice-Hall, 1972), 102.

24. Morris, Conflict *Within the AFL: A Study of Craft versus Industrial Unionism, 1901-1938*, 2.

25. Ibid, 44.

26. Ibid, 2-3.

27. Spero, and Capozzola, The Urban Community and Its Unionized Bureaucracies, 243.

28. Goulden, *Jerry Wurf: Labor's Last Angry Man*, 18.

29. Ibid, 25-39.

30. Ibid, 38

31. Ibid, 54.

32. Ibid, 51.

33. William A. Herbert, "Card Check Certification: Lessons From New York," *Albany Law Review* (2010): 94-173, 129-131.

34. Goulden, Jerry Wurf: Labor's Last Angry Man, 38.

35. Ibid, 63.
36. Ibid, 116.
37. Ibid, 116.
38. Charles A. Krause, "City Workers' Strike Spreads," *Washington Post*, July 8, 1974.
39. Ben A. Franklin, "Baltimore Ends Its 15-Day Strike," *New York Times*, July 15, 1974; Ben A Franklin, "Troopers Patrol Baltimore to Bar Renewed Unrest," New York Times, July 13, 1974.
40. Ibid.
41. Ibid.
42. Jerry Wurf, "Do Police Have the Right to Strike," *Baltimore Sun*, July 20, 1974.
43. Silver, *Forces of Labor: Workers' Movements and Globalization* Since 1870.
44. Murphy, *Blackboard Unions: The AFT and the NEA 1900-1980*, 211.
45. Murphy, "Public Employee Strikes," 74.
46. P.K. Edwards, *Strikes in the United States: 1881-1974* (New York: St. Martin's Press, 1981).

11. MINORITY UNIONISM

1. Rand Wilson and Steve Early, "Back to the Future: Union Survival Strategies in Open Shop America," April 18, 2002, http://talkingunion.wordpress.com/2012/04/18/back-to-the-future-union-survival-strategies-in-open-shop-america/
2. UE News. "Collective Bargaining Rights for Public Employees." https://www.ueunion.org/ue-policy/collective-bargaining-rights-for-public-employees
3. David Selden, *The Teacher Rebellion* (Washington, D.C: Howard University Press, 1985), 16.
4. Ibid, 16.
5. Ibid, 17.
6. Honey, *Going Down Jericho Road: The Memphis Strike, Martin Luther King's Last Campaign*, 65.
7. Ibid, 66-67.
8. Ibid, 68.

9. Ibid, 99.

10. Beifuss, *At the River I Stand: Memphis, The 1968 Strike and Martin Luther King*, 32.

11. McCartin, *Collision Course: Ronald Reagan, The Air Traffic Controllers, and the Strike That Changed America*.

12. Ibid, 95.

13. Ibid, 56.

14. Ibid, 59.

15. Ibid, 59.

16. Josh Eidelson, "Alt-Labor", *The American Prospect*, January 29, 2013, http://prospect.org/article/alt-labor.17. Steven Greenhouse, "At Labor Group, a Sense of a Broader Movement," *New York Times*, September 13, 2013, http://www.nytimes.com/2013/09/14/business/at-afl-cio-a-sense-of-a-broader-labor-movement.html?_r=0

18. Wilson and Early, "Back to the Future: Union Survival Strategies in Open Shop America," 129.

19. Ibid.

20. Institute for Southern Studies, "Amid North Carolina anti-labor campaign, public workers score union win," http://www.southern-studies.org/2013/01/amid-north-carolina-anti-labor-campaign-public-workers-score-union-win.html.

21. Ibid.

22. "What We've Accomplished," UE Local, http://www.ue150.org/150about_accomplished.html.

23. Steve Early, "House of Labor Needs Repairs, Not Just New Roommates," *Labor Notes*, September 16, 2014, http://www.labor-notes.org/2013/09/house-labor-needs-repairs-not-just-new-roommates#sthash.TNXfQiJa.dpuf

CONCLUSION

1. Supreme Court of the United States, "Janus v. American Federation of State, County, and Municipal Employees, Council 31, et al." https://www.supremecourt.gov/opinions/17pdf/16-1466_2b3j.pdf

2. Lindsay Colvin Stone, "Supreme Court Deems Public-Sector Union Agency Fees Unconstitutional." Labor and Employment

Law Blog, June 28, 2018. https://www.laboremploymentlawblog.
com/2018/06/articles/scotus/public-sector-union-agency-fees-
unconstitutional/

3. Adam Liptak, "Supreme Court Ruling Delivers a Sharp Blow
to Labor Unions," *New York Times*, June 27, 2018. https://www.
nytimes.com/2018/06/27/us/politics/supreme-court-unions-orga-
nized-labor.html

4. *Janus v. American Federation of State, County, and Municipal Employees, Council 31, et al.*

5. Jen Kirby, "Elena Kagan's dissent trashes Supreme Court as 'black-
robed rulers overriding citizens' choices'" *Vox*, June 27, 2018.
https://www.vox.com/2018/6/27/17510338/supreme-court-kagan-
dissent-janus

6. James Gray Pope, Ed Bruno, Peter Kellman, "It's Time for Unions
To Let Go of Exclusive Representation," *In These Times*, July 19,
2018. http://inthesetimes.com/features/unions_exclusive_represen-
tation_janus.html

7. AFSCME, "Preserving Exclusive Representation," https://www.
afscme.org/members/conventions/resolutions-and-amend-
ments/2018/resolutions/58-preserving-exclusive-representation

8. Cherrene Horazuk, "Viewpoint: Unions Aren't Exclusive Clubs—
We Fight for All Workers," *Labor Notes*, August 17, 2018. http://
labornotes.org/blogs/2018/08/viewpoint-unions-arent-exclusive-
clubs-we-fight-all-workers

9. Lee Saunders, "A Union Response to the Supreme Court's
Janus Decision, *American Prospect*, Juny 9, 2018. http://
prospect.org/article/union-response-supreme-courts-janus-
decision?fbclid=IwAR08ct-icXGENaeA1IS5gl608GFrJTJiDXYu-
BrpHottV93NZdXI5Z1OoSdg

10. Sally Ho, "Strike ending for last Washington teachers still picketing," *Seattle Times*, September 17, 2018. https://www.seattletimes.
com/seattle-news/education/with-deal-reached-in-tumwater-all-
washington-teacher-contract-conflicts-settled/